designer's guide to color

3

BY IKUYOSHI SHIBUKAWA *AND* YUMI TAKAHASHI

INTRODUCTORY ESSAY *BY*
JEANNE ALLEN

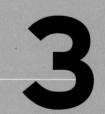

CHRONICLE BOOKS
SAN FRANCISCO

THIS EDITION PUBLISHED IN 2007 BY CHRONICLE BOOKS LLC.

ENGLISH TEXT COPYRIGHT © 1986 BY CHRONICLE BOOKS.
COPYRIGHT © 1986 BY KAWADE SHOBO SHINSHA.
ALL RIGHTS RESERVED. NO PART OF THIS BOOK MAY BE REPRODUCED IN ANY
FORM WITHOUT WRITTEN PERMISSION FROM THE PUBLISHER.

HAISHOKU JITEN BY IKUYOSHI SHIBUKAWA AND YUMI TAKAHASHI WAS FIRST
PUBLISHED IN JAPAN BY KAWADE SHOBO SHINSHA PUBLISHERS.

ISBN-10: 0-8118-5706-9
ISBN-13: 978-0-8118-5706-2

THE LIBRARY OF CONGRESS HAS CATALOGED THE PREVIOUS EDITION
AS FOLLOWS:

ALLEN, JEANNE, 1945-
DESIGNER'S GUIDE TO COLOR 3.
BASED ON *HAISHOKU JITEN* BY IKUYOSHI SHIBUKAWA
AND YUMI TAKAHASHI, 1986.
1. COLOR IN ART. 2. COLOR. 3. PSYCHOLOGICAL ASPECTS.
I. SHIBUKAWA, IKUYOSHI. HAISHOKU JITEN II. TITLE. III.
TITLE: *DESIGNER'S GUIDE TO COLOR 3.*
ND 1488.A44 1986
701.'8 86-17558
ISBN: 0-87701-415-9
ISBN: 0-87701-408-6 (PAPERBACK)

MANUFACTURED IN JAPAN.

DISTRIBUTED IN CANADA BY RAINCOAST BOOKS
9050 SHAUGHNESSY STREET
VANCOUVER, BRITISH COLUMBIA V6P 6E5

10 9 8 7 6 5 4 3 2 1

CHRONICLE BOOKS LLC
680 SECOND STREET
SAN FRANCISCO, CALIFORNIA 94107

WWW.CHRONICLEBOOKS.COM

Contents

Introduction

For anyone working in any aspect of design — from architecture to interiors and graphics to fashion — combining color is an agonizing process of trial and error. Certainly some designers are gifted with perfect color pitch, but for the rest of us, the mind's eye is an illusive, unsettled place. We all "know it when we see it," but creating "it" from scratch is a problematic process.

Excellent books on color theory and use have been written by such authors as Johannes Itten and Luigina De Grandis. These complex, sophisticated works, although they are important source books for anyone seriously involved with color, show *why* color works as it does, but not *how* to use it.

Designer's Guide to Color 3, on the other hand, teaches its visually oriented audience through illustrated examples — the language designers understand best. This colorful and compact handbook, never pretending to compete with the scientific approach of Itten and De Grandis, shows how colors work together and uses just enough of the written word to satisfy the intellect.

My own experience with this book probably best describes its value. When I began to write the text that accompanies the illustrations, I was also designing prints for a new dress collection. The design work involved developing new color directions — as well as coloring the same pattern differently to achieve radically different color moods — and I quite naturally began to use the book's illustrations to test my ideas. Because it is organized in the same way that designers work — with anywhere from six to sixty different colorations of the same pattern — the book can be called user-friendly in the truest sense.

Midway through both the designing and the writing, I introduced *Designer's Guide to Color 3* to my assistant and the Japanese textile artists who prepare our work for printing. We all discovered that we used the book to inspire new ideas and to visualize the ways specific colors would appear in any pattern, from a simple dot to a complicated floral. Quite apart from the book (but because of it), we were able to develop new color combinations by duplicating tonalities, using an entirely different color range. Also, the bock's creative use of accent color contributes invaluable visual suggestions that can bring otherwise dull compositions to life.

By the time our print collection was finished, we had neatly integrated the book into our everyday work. *Designer's Guide to Color 3* encourages all designers to try something new and to see the familiar in a new way. The appealing patterns and colorations are as delightful as they are informative, making this book a pleasure in every sense of the word.

How to Use This Book

The best way to use this book is to begin at the beginning. *Designer's Guide to Color 3* is a progressive study of the way colors combine to create patterns, starting with simple two-color dots and systematically building to baroque multicolored floral combinations and beyond. Brief descriptions accompany the patterns and highlight the important points of each design.

The book is loosely organized by type of pattern. After the simple geometrics come stripes, checks, plaids, a variety of print subjects (including abstracts, florals, landscapes), art deco, paisley, and traditional Japanese patterns, among others. The patterns are presented in a manner meant to graphically illustrate the power of color and design in conveying a profound visual message.

As you move from pattern to pattern, read the descriptions to train and test your eye, and you will begin to recognize why certain color combinations have a particular impact and how different colors can make the same pattern look strikingly different.

Color chips are shown at the right of each example for anyone interested in reproducing the colors illustrated. The chips represent the colors used in each design (not including white). As in the first two books in this series, tint values for each color are also shown. The colors are produced by combining the tint values of the four basic print colors: *Y* stands for yellow, *M* for magenta, *C* for cyan, and *BL* for black. Color percentages are also given, but remember that inks, papers, presses, and printing techniques vary from country to country, and the recipes are not infallible.

The designer can use this book to study the subjects of complementary color, tonal values, and the effects of contrast and perspective in a variety of patterns and designs. But this book can also be a source of enjoyment and visual pleasure for anyone who appreciates beautiful combinations of pattern and color.

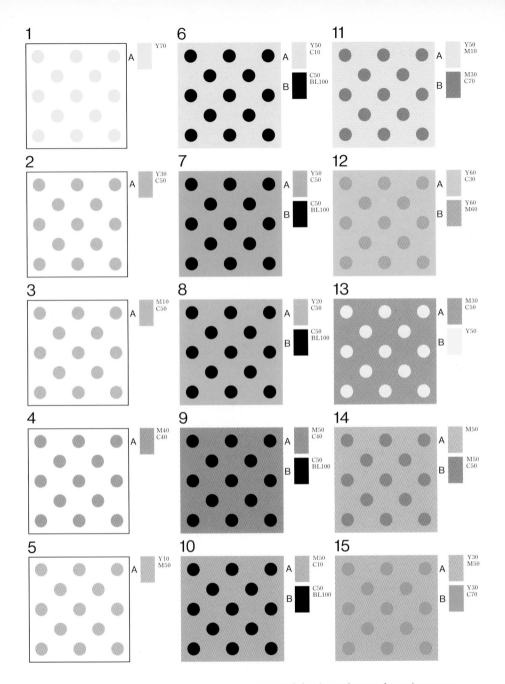

1 A — Y70

6 A — Y50 C10 / B — C50 BL100

11 A — Y50 M10 / B — M30 C70

2 A — Y30 C50

7 A — Y50 C50 / B — C50 BL100

12 A — Y60 C30 / B — Y60 M60

3 A — M10 C50

8 A — Y20 C50 / B — C50 BL100

13 A — M30 C50 / B — Y50

4 A — M40 C40

9 A — M50 C40 / B — C50 BL100

14 A — M50 / B — M50 C50

5 A — Y10 M50

10 A — M50 C10 / B — C50 BL100

15 A — Y30 M50 / B — Y30 C70

Dots

Always modern and fresh, dots can be styled in numerous ways: By altering the size from small (pin) dots to large (balloon) dots; by scattering them randomly, rather than arranging them in evenly spaced, horizontal rows; by using more than one color. On these pages, small (pin) dots are presented in their most basic form: two-colored, evenly spaced patterns. A simple change to this pattern, however, can generate remarkable

4

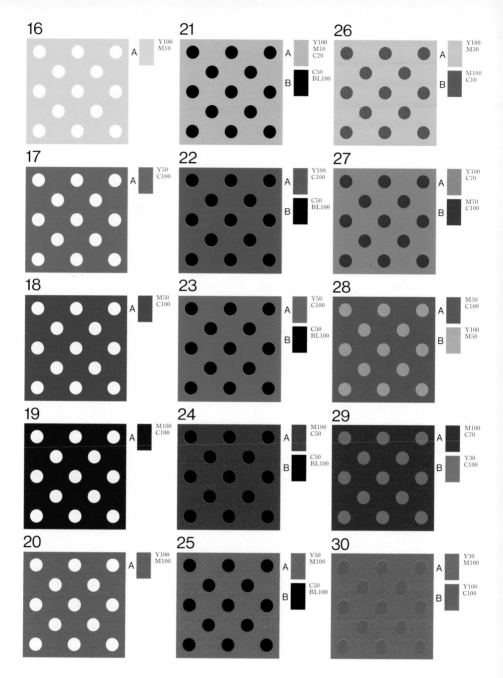

No.	A	B
16	Y100 M10	
17	Y50 C100	
18	M50 C100	
19	M100 C100	
20	Y100 M100	
21	Y100 M10 C20	C50 BL100
22	Y100 C100	C50 BL100
23	Y50 C100	C50 BL100
24	M100 C50	C50 BL100
25	Y50 M100	C50 BL100
26	Y100 M30	M100 C10
27	Y100 C70	M70 C100
28	M30 C100	Y100 M50
29	M100 C70	Y30 C100
30	Y30 M100	Y100 C100

diversity.

Pale, clear colors on a white background (examples 1-5) are clean and cool with a fresh, transparent quality. In examples 6-10, black dots on bright, clear colors create a slick, stylish mood from the licorice All Sorts image.

Although white dots on vivid brights (examples 16-20) broadcast a clean, vital, sporty message, black dots (examples 21-25) project an aggressive, urban feeling; these dark brights are almost preda-

5

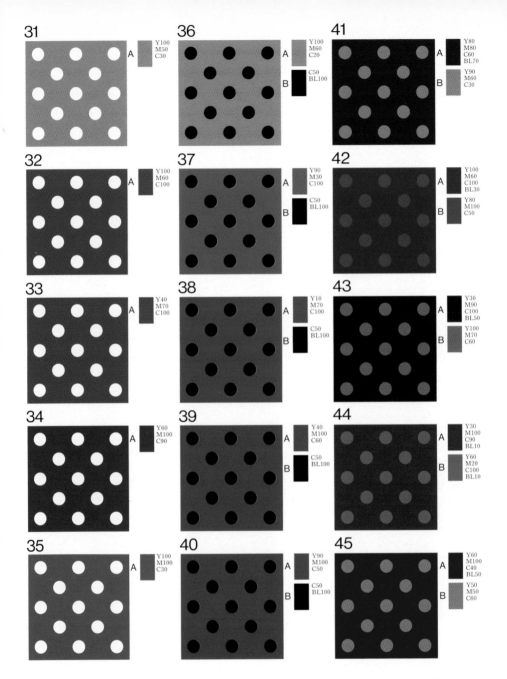

31
A — Y100 M50 C30

36
A — Y100 M60 C20
B — C50 BL100

41
A — Y80 M80 C60 BL70
B — Y90 M60 C30

32
A — Y100 M60 C100

37
A — Y90 M30 C100
B — C50 BL100

42
A — Y100 M60 C100 BL30
B — Y80 M100 C50

33
A — Y40 M70 C100

38
A — Y10 M70 C100
B — C50 BL100

43
A — Y30 M90 C100 BL50
B — Y100 M70 C60

34
A — Y60 M100 C90

39
A — Y40 M100 C60
B — C50 BL100

44
A — Y30 M100 C90 BL10
B — Y60 M20 C100 BL10

35
A — Y100 M100 C30

40
A — Y90 M100 C50
B — C50 BL100

45
A — Y60 M100 C40 BL50
B — Y50 M50 C60

tory. Complementary combinations of bright dots on brilliant backgrounds (examples 26-30) create a carnival mood exploding with vitality, good humor, and fun.

Example 31 begins a shift to dark, sub-

dued backgrounds. Examples 41-45 have a rich, luxurious quality reminiscent of autumn moods and country life. Deep, dark color tones prevail in examples 46-60. Black dots on dusty tones of taupe, blue, burgundy, and umber in examples

6

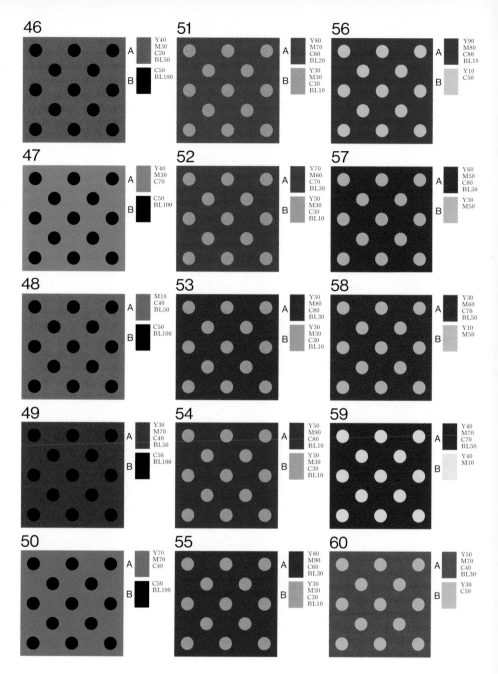

46
A Y40 M30 C20 BL50
B C50 BL100

51
A Y80 M70 C60 BL20
B Y30 M30 C30 BL10

56
A Y90 M80 C80 BL10
B Y10 C50

47
A Y40 M30 C70
B C50 BL100

52
A Y70 M60 C70 BL30
B Y30 M30 C30 BL10

57
A Y60 M50 C80 BL50
B Y30 M50

48
A M10 C40 BL50
B C50 BL100

53
A Y30 M80 C80 BL30
B Y30 M30 C30 BL10

58
A Y30 M60 C70 BL50
B Y10 M50

49
A Y30 M70 C40 BL50
B C50 BL100

54
A Y50 M90 C80 BL10
B Y30 M30 C30 BL10

59
A Y40 M70 C70 BL50
B Y40 M10

50
A Y70 M70 C40
B C50 BL100

55
A Y80 M90 C60 BL30
B Y30 M30 C30 BL10

60
A Y50 M70 C40 BL30
B Y30 C50

46-50 have a subdued, masculine image. Gray dots (examples 51-55) are in soft contrast to the darker base colors, creating a comfortable harmony between the dots and the background. In examples 56-60, the mood changes dramatically when dusty pink or yellow dots replace the neutral grays.

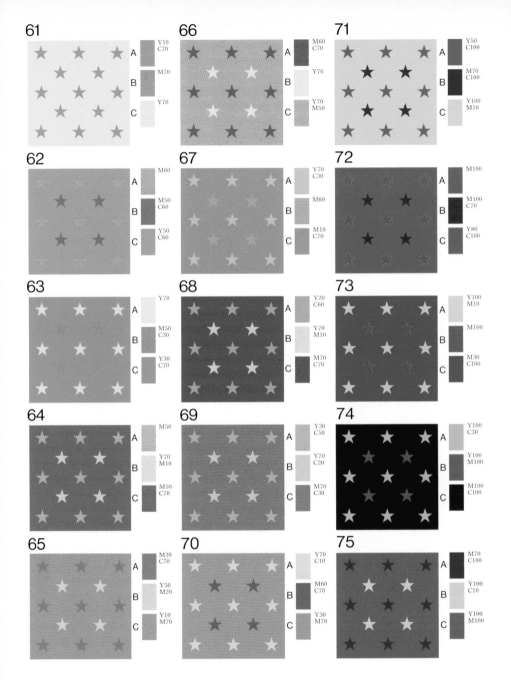

61	**66**	**71**
A — Y10 C70	A — M60 C70	A — Y50 C100
B — M70	B — Y70	B — M70 C100
C — Y70	C — Y70 M50	C — Y100 M10
62	**67**	**72**
A — M60	A — Y70 C30	A — M100
B — M50 C60	B — M60	B — M100 C70
C — Y50 C60	C — M10 C70	C — Y80 C100
63	**68**	**73**
A — Y70	A — Y20 C60	A — Y100 M10
B — M50 C30	B — Y70 M10	B — M100
C — Y30 C70	C — M70 C70	C — M30 C100
64	**69**	**74**
A — M50	A — Y30 C50	A — Y100 C30
B — Y70 M10	B — Y70 C20	B — Y100 M100
C — M50 C70	C — M70 C30	C — M100 C100
65	**70**	**75**
A — M30 C70	A — Y70 C10	A — M70 C100
B — Y50 M20	B — M60 C70	B — Y100 C10
C — Y10 M70	C — Y30 M70	C — Y100 M100

Stars

This alternating star pattern is more whimsical and more complex than the two-color dot design. The bright pastel tones with medium brights (examples 61-65) create a young, soft image — perfect for children's clothing and toys. Examples 66-70 show unusual, sophisticated, feminine tones typical of teenage fashion. Primary and secondary colors (examples 71-75) create a "popping" effect reminiscent of pop art from the sixties.

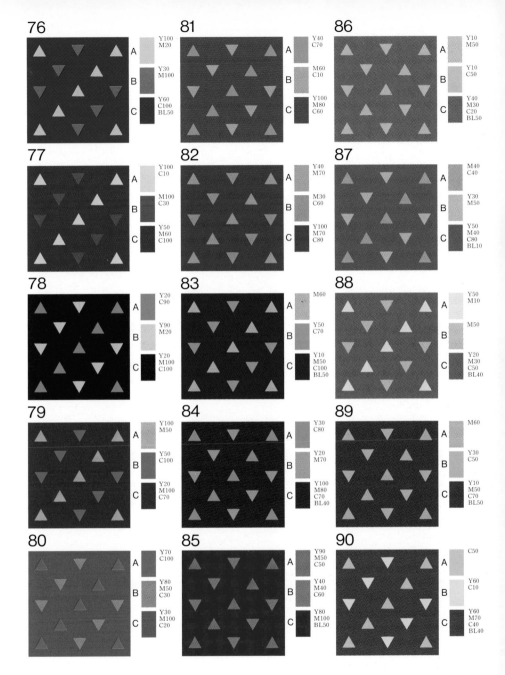

Triangles

The diagonal stripe pattern that emerges by alternating the triangle colors gives this design a modern but stable feeling. Triangles colored randomly or horizontally would create an entirely different effect. The "popping" color in examples 76-80 creates a tension with the more subdued colors and emphasizes the diagonal stripe. Chalky pastels on gray (examples 86-90) create patterns reminiscent of Early American quilts.

9

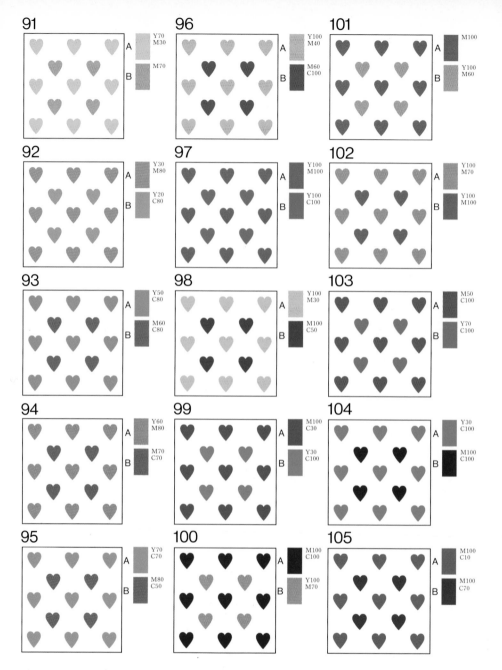

| 91 | A | Y70 M30 |
| | B | M70 |

| 92 | A | Y30 M80 |
| | B | Y20 C80 |

| 93 | A | Y50 C80 |
| | B | M60 C80 |

| 94 | A | Y60 M80 |
| | B | M70 C70 |

| 95 | A | Y70 C70 |
| | B | M80 C50 |

| 96 | A | Y100 M40 |
| | B | M60 C100 |

| 97 | A | Y100 M100 |
| | B | Y100 C100 |

| 98 | A | Y100 M30 |
| | B | M100 C50 |

| 99 | A | M100 C30 |
| | B | Y30 C100 |

| 100 | A | M100 C100 |
| | B | Y100 M70 |

| 101 | A | M100 |
| | B | Y100 M60 |

| 102 | A | Y100 M70 |
| | B | Y100 M100 |

| 103 | A | M50 C100 |
| | B | Y70 C100 |

| 104 | A | Y30 C100 |
| | B | M100 C100 |

| 105 | A | M100 C10 |
| | B | M100 C70 |

Card Suits

In examples 91-105, hearts are shown in alternating horizontal stripes of color on a white background. Even though various color combinations are used in these examples, any difference in per-sonality in these examples is minor; the white background is so dominant that all the combinations seem graphic, clean, and bright. A change in the base color would dramatically alter the effect.

In examples 106-120, clubs, diamonds,

10

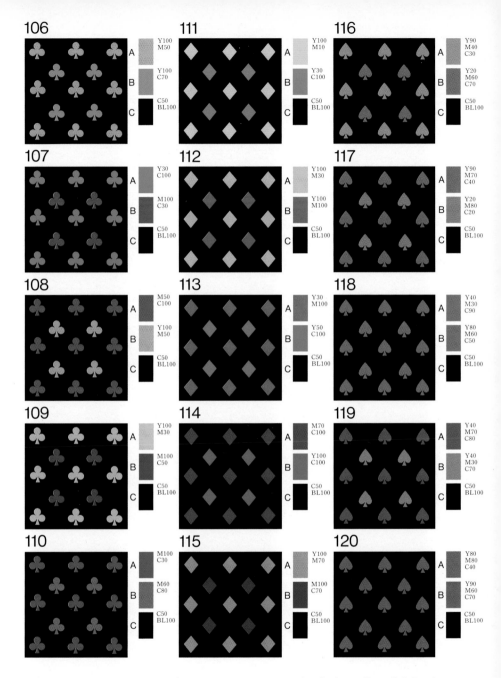

and spades are shown against a black background. Again, the background is so dominant that all the combinations assume a similar personality — in this case, aggressive, tense, and chic. Bright, vivid colors on black (examples 106-115) cre-

ate a stained-glass effect. Subdued colors (examples 116-120) contrast tonally to create a calm harmony.

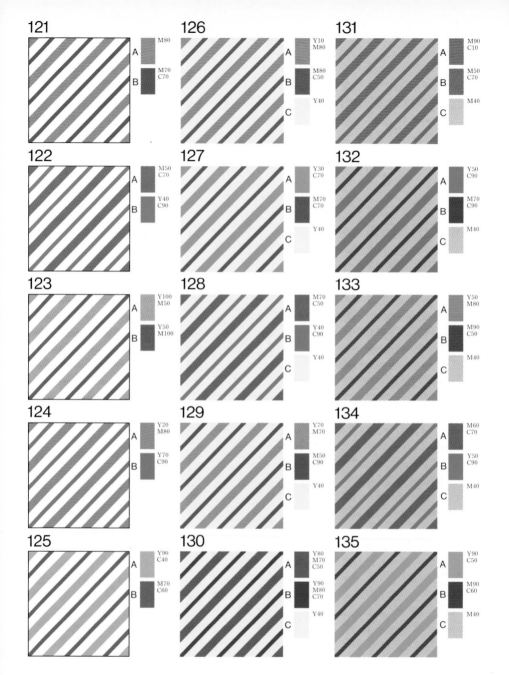

Alternate Stripes (1)

Depending on color and juxtaposition, two diagonal stripes of different sizes can create entirely different effects. At first, the examples on these pages seem to show a variety of stripe sizes and patterns — in fact, except for the colors, the examples are identical.

As with the card suits, the white background is the dominant force in examples 121-125. In examples 126-130, the yellow base color softens the design and

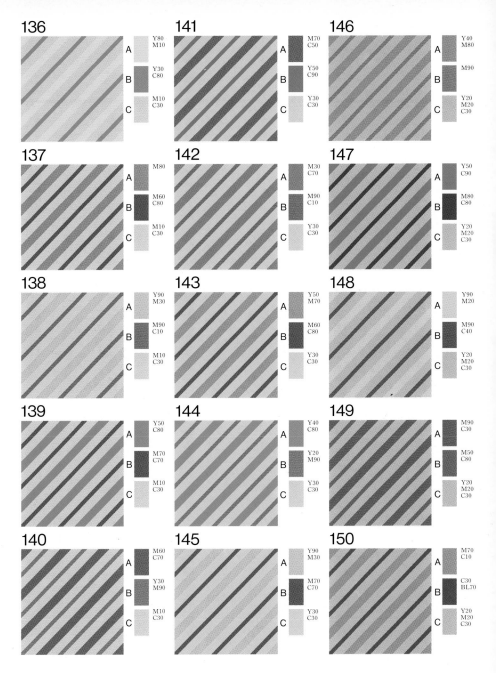

encourages the wide stripe to prevail. The pink background (examples 131-135) gives the design a distinctively feminine character and a graphic strength that is settled, disciplined, and appealing. Unlike examples 121-145, which demand at- tention by using contrasting colors, examples 146-150 use a neutral gray background for a cool, calm effect.

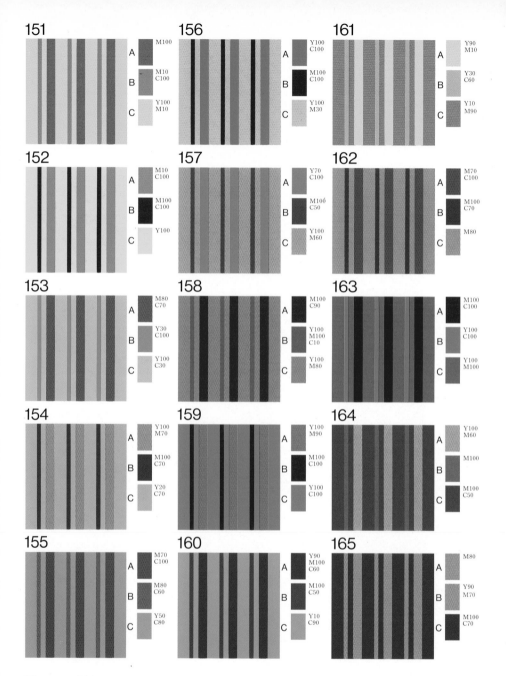

Alternate Stripes (2)

These two stripes have the same design relationship as the stripes on the previous pages. These examples, however, create a completely different impression because the stripes run vertically, not diagonally. Vertical stripes are stronger and more grounded than kinetic diagonal stripes. As a result, the contrasting colors used here have a contained boldness that makes this "awning stripe" design a classic in everything from lawn

14

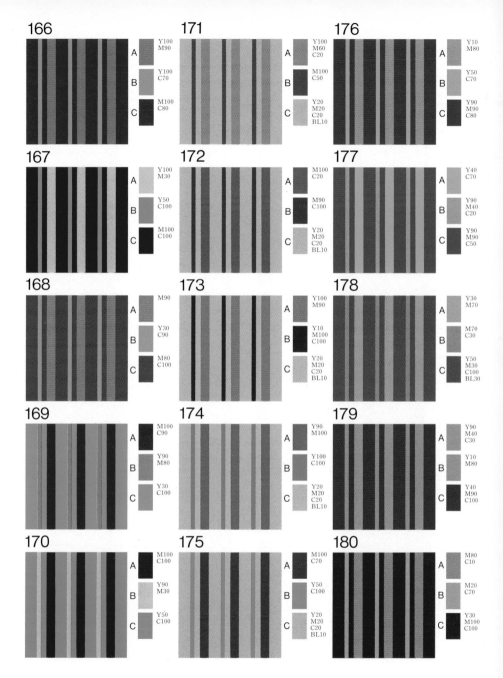

166
A — Y100 M90
B — Y100 C70
C — M100 C80

167
A — Y100 M30
B — Y50 C100
C — M100 C100

168
A — M90
B — Y30 C90
C — M80 C100

169
A — M100 C90
B — Y90 M80
C — Y30 C100

170
A — M100 C100
B — Y90 M30
C — Y50 C100

171
A — Y100 M60 C20
B — M100 C50
C — Y20 M20 C20 BL10

172
A — M100 C20
B — M90 C100
C — Y20 M20 C20 BL10

173
A — Y100 M90
B — Y10 M100 C100
C — Y20 M20 C20 BL10

174
A — Y90 M100
B — Y100 C100
C — Y20 M20 C20 BL10

175
A — M100 C70
B — Y50 C100
C — Y20 M20 C20 BL10

176
A — Y10 M80
B — Y50 C70
C — Y90 M90 C80

177
A — Y40 C70
B — Y90 M40 C20
C — Y90 M90 C50

178
A — Y30 M70
B — M70 C30
C — Y50 M30 C100 BL30

179
A — Y90 M40 C30
B — Y10 M80
C — Y40 M90 C100

180
A — M80 C10
B — M20 C70
C — Y30 M100 C100

chairs to wrapping paper.

Double stripes on bright, vivid backgrounds (examples 151-170) suggest bold summer colors. Even with subdued colors (example 155), the contrast of hue suggests a cool (but not cold) sophistica-

tion. A staid quality creeps into the design with the neutral base in examples 171-175; the stripe is more controlled, and gaiety has been replaced by measured "good taste."

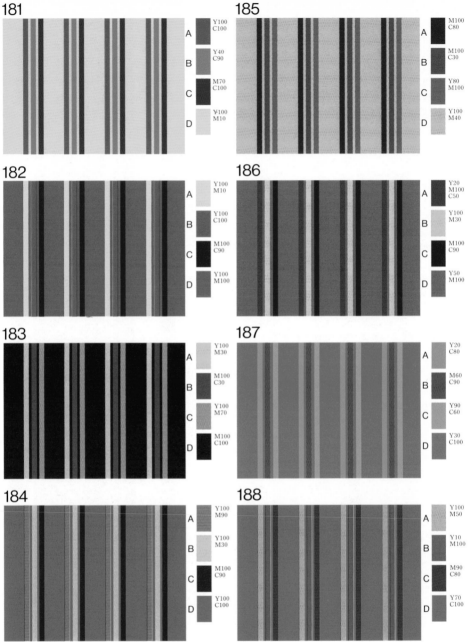

181

A	Y100 C100
B	Y40 C90
C	M70 C100
D	Y100 M10

185

A	M100 C80
B	M100 C30
C	Y80 M100
D	Y100 M40

182

A	Y100 M10
B	Y100 C100
C	M100 C90
D	Y100 M100

186

A	Y20 M100 C50
B	Y100 M30
C	M100 C90
D	Y50 M100

183

A	Y100 M30
B	M100 C30
C	Y100 M70
D	M100 C100

187

A	Y20 C80
B	M60 C90
C	Y90 C60
D	Y30 C100

184

A	Y100 M90
B	Y100 M30
C	M100 C90
D	Y100 C100

188

A	Y100 M50
B	Y10 M100
C	M90 C80
D	Y70 C100

Triple Stripes

Careful selection and placement of color in this design gives each color a completely different character from example to example. Blue, for instance, appears in every example here, but only example 187 *seems* blue. Although the examples have much in common — the regularity of the design spacing and the consistent use of bright color — the attention to juxtaposition gives each a distinct character.

16

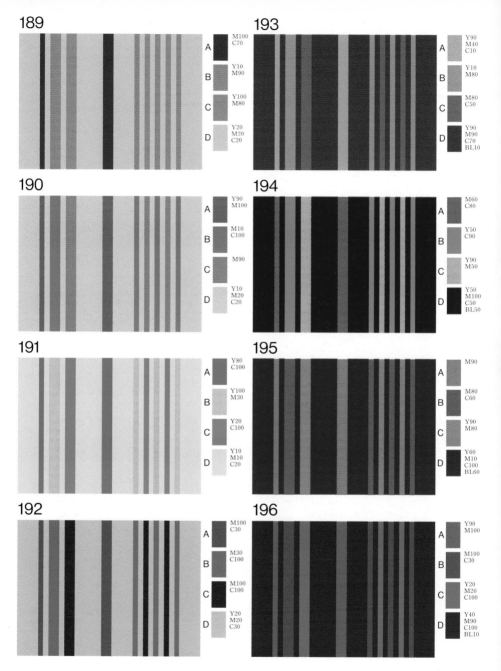

189

A — M100 C70
B — Y10 M90
C — Y100 M80
D — Y20 M20 C20

190

A — Y90 M100
B — M10 C100
C — M90
D — Y10 M20 C20

191

A — Y80 C100
B — Y100 M30
C — Y20 C100
D — Y10 M10 C20

192

A — M100 C30
B — M30 C100
C — M100 C100
D — Y20 M20 C30

193

A — Y90 M40 C10
B — Y10 M80
C — M80 C50
D — Y90 M90 C70 BL10

194

A — M60 C80
B — Y50 C90
C — Y90 M50
D — Y50 M100 C50 BL50

195

A — M90
B — M80 C60
C — Y90 M80
D — Y60 M10 C100 BL60

196

A — Y90 M100
B — M100 C30
C — Y20 M20 C100
D — Y40 M90 C100 BL10

Irregular Stripes

This pattern uses randomly placed stripes and consistent color rotation (the placement of A, B, C, and D) to create unique examples of the same design. Bright stripes on a gray background (ex-amples 189-192) jump forward in a free and easy rhythm. By comparison, the same vivid stripes on a deep, saturated color base (examples 193-196) seem con-tained and controlled.

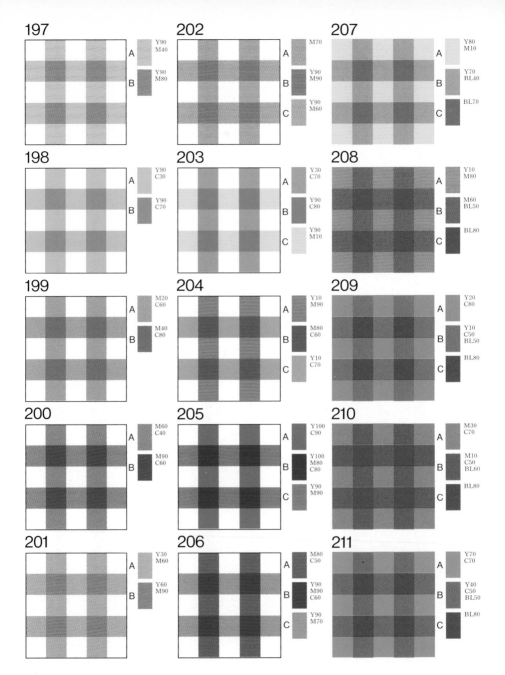

197
A — Y90 M40
B — Y90 M80

202
A — M70
B — Y90 M90
C — Y90 M60

207
A — Y80 M10
B — Y70 BL40
C — BL70

198
A — Y90 C30
B — Y90 C70

203
A — Y30 C70
B — Y90 C80
C — Y90 M10

208
A — Y10 M80
B — M60 BL50
C — BL80

199
A — M20 C60
B — M40 C80

204
A — Y10 M90
B — M80 C60
C — Y10 C70

209
A — Y20 C80
B — Y10 C50 BL50
C — BL80

200
A — M60 C40
B — M90 C60

205
A — Y100 C90
B — Y100 M80 C80
C — Y90 M90

210
A — M30 C70
B — M10 C50 BL60
C — BL80

201
A — Y30 M60
B — Y60 M90

206
A — M80 C50
B — Y90 M90 C60
C — Y90 M70

211
A — Y70 C70
B — Y40 C50 BL50
C — BL80

Gingham Checks (1)

The gingham check — according to the movies, a popular design for pioneer women of the Old West — is one of the simplest of the yarn-dyed designs. The warp yarn of one color and the weft yarn of another color cross in a regular pattern to create a third, pure color. (The color created by the crossing of the warp and weft yarn colors is said to be

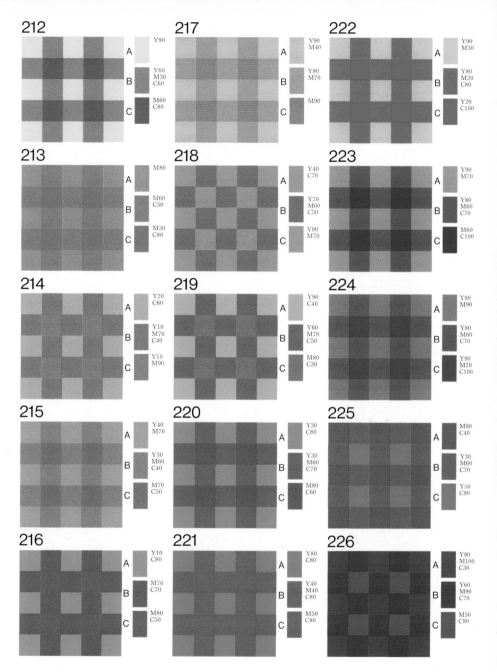

212
- A: Y90
- B: Y60 M30 C60
- C: M60 C80

217
- A: Y90 M40
- B: Y80 M70
- C: M90

222
- A: Y90 M30
- B: Y80 M20 C80
- C: Y20 C100

213
- A: M80
- B: M60 C50
- C: M30 C80

218
- A: Y40 C70
- B: Y70 M60 C50
- C: Y90 M70

223
- A: Y90 M70
- B: Y80 M60 C70
- C: M60 C100

214
- A: Y20 C60
- B: Y10 M70 C40
- C: Y10 M90

219
- A: Y90 C40
- B: Y60 M70 C50
- C: M80 C30

224
- A: Y90 M90
- B: Y80 M60 C70
- C: Y90 M20 C100

215
- A: Y40 M70
- B: Y30 M60 C40
- C: M70 C50

220
- A: Y30 C80
- B: Y30 M60 C70
- C: M80 C60

225
- A: M90 C40
- B: Y30 M60 C70
- C: Y50 C90

216
- A: Y10 C80
- B: M70 C70
- C: M80 C50

221
- A: Y80 C80
- B: Y40 M40 C80
- C: M50 C80

226
- A: Y80 M100 C30
- B: Y60 M90 C70
- C: M50 C90

"chambrayed.") In example 203, for instance, blue and yellow cross to create green. The green is very intense because, unlike the blue and yellow, it is not mixed with the base color, white.

The provocative combinations in examples 212-226 expand the traditional definition of gingham check and seem more modern art than gingham.

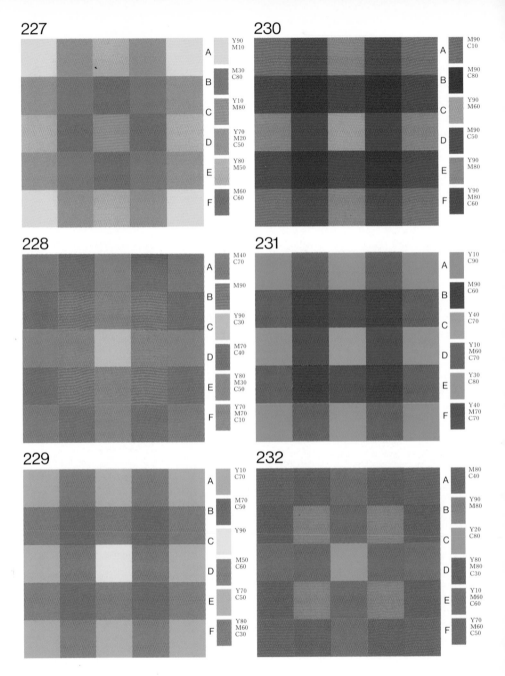

227

A	Y90 M10
B	M30 C80
C	Y10 M80
D	Y70 M20 C50
E	Y80 M50
F	M60 C60

230

A	M90 C10
B	M90 C80
C	Y90 M60
D	M90 C50
E	Y90 M80
F	Y90 M80 C60

228

A	M40 C70
B	M90
C	Y90 C30
D	M70 C40
E	Y80 M30 C50
F	Y70 M70 C10

231

A	Y10 C90
B	M90 C60
C	Y40 C70
D	Y10 M60 C70
E	Y30 C80
F	Y40 M70 C70

229

A	Y10 C70
B	M70 C50
C	Y90
D	M50 C60
E	Y70 C50
F	Y80 M60 C30

232

A	M80 C40
B	Y90 M80
C	Y20 C80
D	Y80 M80 C30
E	Y10 M60 C60
F	Y70 M60 C50

Gingham Checks (2)

These examples, more complicated than examples 197-226, use three colors for each of the vertical and horizontal stripes. Because colors combine in an unpredictable way, plaid designs such as these are difficult to execute. When designing yarn-dyed textiles, the designer paints a representation of the *intended* result, which often differs greatly from the *actual* result because paper and cloth are such different mediums.

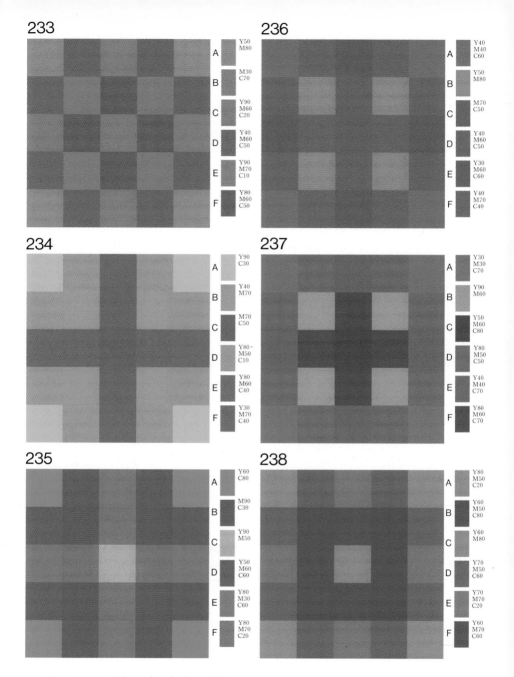

233

A — Y50 M80
B — M30 C70
C — Y90 M60 C20
D — Y40 M60 C50
E — Y90 M70 C10
F — Y80 M60 C50

236

A — Y40 M40 C60
B — Y50 M80
C — M70 C50
D — Y40 M60 C50
E — Y30 M60 C60
F — Y40 M70 C40

234

A — Y90 C30
B — Y40 M70
C — M70 C50
D — Y80 M50 C10
E — Y80 M60 C40
F — Y30 M70 C40

237

A — Y30 M30 C70
B — Y90 M60
C — Y50 M60 C80
D — Y80 M50 C50
E — Y40 M40 C70
F — Y80 M60 C70

235

A — Y60 C80
B — M90 C30
C — Y90 M50
D — Y50 M60 C60
E — Y80 M30 C60
F — Y80 M70 C20

238

A — Y80 M50 C20
B — Y60 M50 C80
C — Y60 M80
D — Y70 M50 C60
E — Y70 M70 C20
F — Y60 M70 C60

To understand how the design was created, study the color percentages to the right of each example. Depending on the colors selected to mix, each example has a distinct color personality.

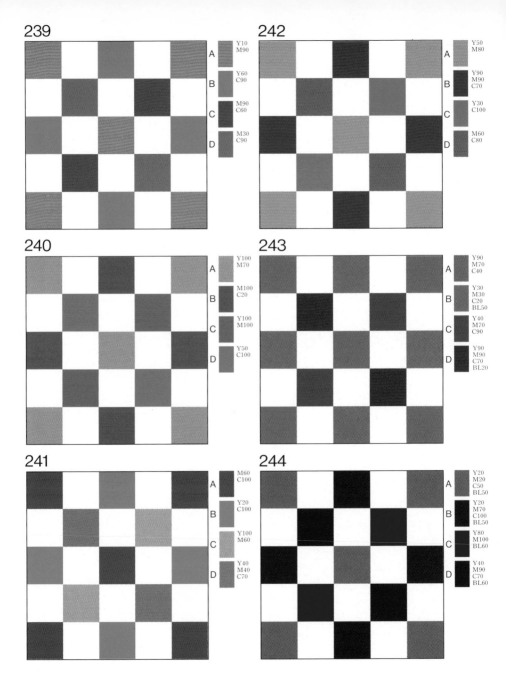

239

A — Y10 M90
B — Y60 C90
C — M90 C60
D — M30 C90

242

A — Y50 M80
B — Y90 M90 C70
C — Y30 C100
D — M60 C80

240

A — Y100 M70
B — M100 C20
C — Y100 M100
D — Y50 C100

243

A — Y90 M70 C40
B — Y30 M30 C20 BL50
C — Y40 M70 C90
D — Y90 M90 C70 BL20

241

A — M60 C100
B — Y20 C100
C — Y100 M60
D — Y40 M40 C70

244

A — Y20 M20 C50 BL50
B — Y20 M70 C100 BL50
C — Y80 M100 BL60
D — Y40 M90 C70 BL60

Block Checks

This pattern, although identical to the gingham check pattern on the previous pages, looks totally different because the colors are pure, with none of the chambrayed effect of merged color. The tile-

22

like design, popularly known in Japan as *ichimatsu mōyo,* is simple and modern and can use numerous color combinations successfully.

The effect of combining bright, vivid color on a white base (examples 239-241)

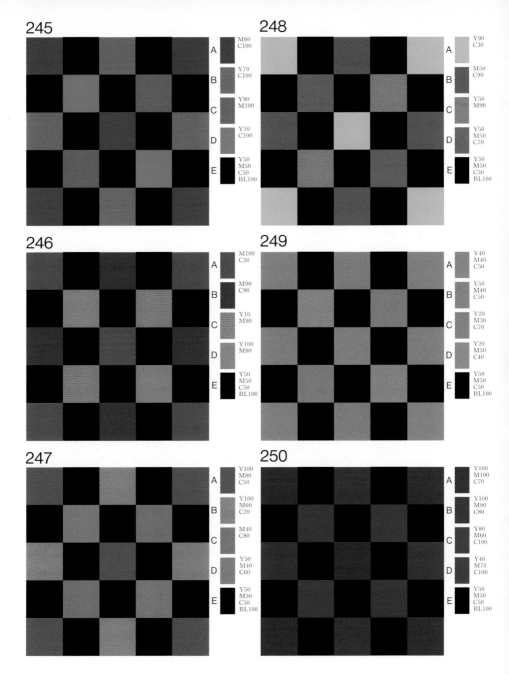

is clean and cheerful. The more subdued colors on white in examples 242-244 create a conservative image but retain a light, clean feel because of the high percentage of white used. Examples 245-250 replace the white background with black and exude a deep, saturated intensity of color that draws the viewer into the design.

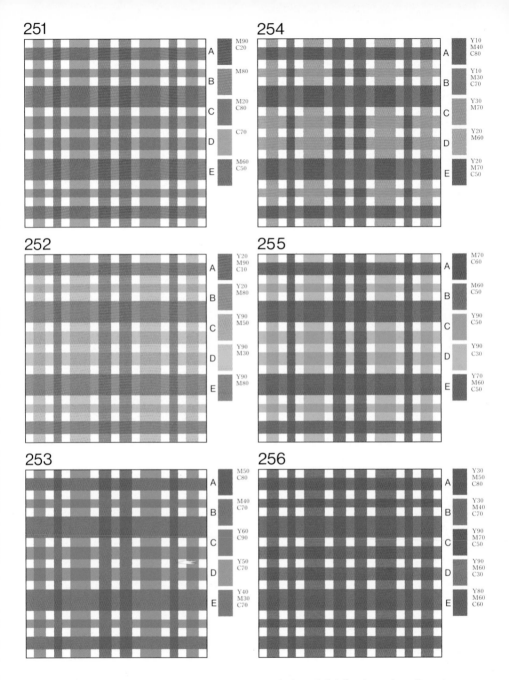

251

A	M90 C20
B	M80
C	M20 C80
D	C70
E	M60 C50

254

A	Y10 M40 C80
B	Y10 M30 C70
C	Y30 M70
D	Y20 M60
E	Y20 M70 C50

252

A	Y20 M90 C10
B	Y20 M80
C	Y90 M50
D	Y90 M30
E	Y90 M80

255

A	M70 C60
B	M60 C50
C	Y90 C50
D	Y90 C30
E	Y70 M60 C50

253

A	M50 C80
B	M40 C70
C	Y60 C90
D	Y50 C70
E	Y40 M30 C70

256

A	Y30 M50 C80
B	Y30 M40 C70
C	Y90 M70 C50
D	Y90 M60 C30
E	Y80 M60 C60

Madras Plaids

This plaid originated in India, where it was woven into cotton and used for clothing and for textiles used in interior decoration. Now popular everywhere, the madras plaid design has become a

wardrobe cliché for the university set. Vertical and horizontal threads create mixed color blocks of varied sizes in this design. Examples 251-256 are rather atypical colorings for this plaid — beige is a more common base color than white

24

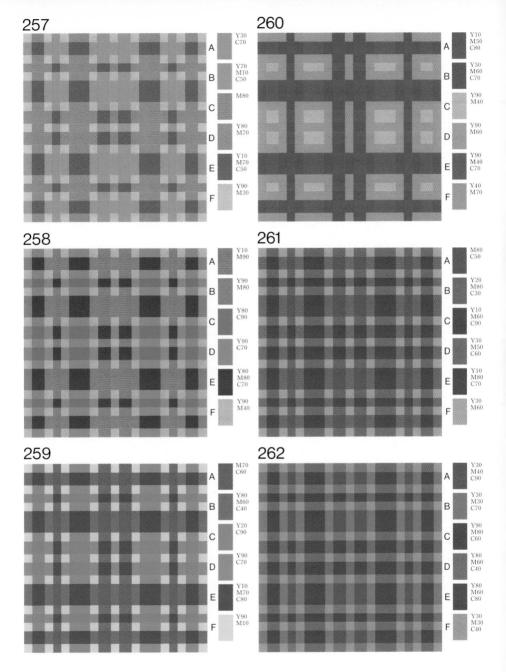

257

A — Y30 C70
B — Y70 M10 C50
C — M80
D — Y80 M70
E — Y10 M70 C50
F — Y90 M30

260

A — Y10 M50 C80
B — Y30 M60 C70
C — Y90 M40
D — Y90 M60
E — Y90 M40 C70
F — Y40 M70

258

A — Y10 M90
B — Y90 M80
C — Y80 C90
D — Y90 C70
E — Y80 M80 C70
F — Y90 M40

261

A — M80 C50
B — Y20 M80 C30
C — Y10 M60 C90
D — Y30 M50 C60
E — Y10 M80 C70
F — Y30 M60

259

A — M70 C60
B — Y80 M60 C40
C — Y20 C90
D — Y90 C70
E — Y10 M70 C80
F — Y90 M10

262

A — Y30 M40 C90
B — Y30 M30 C70
C — Y90 M80 C60
D — Y80 M60 C40
E — Y80 M60 C80
F — Y30 M30 C40

—but the limited use of color on white has a clean, refreshing look. Examples 257-261 are more typical of madras patterns. Example 257 is tonal and harmonious, due in part to the gold background; example 259, because of the bright yel-

low background, is far more intense.

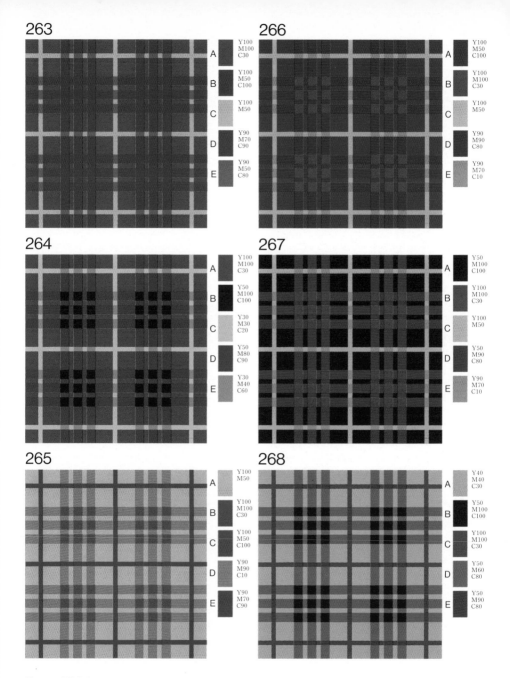

Tartan Plaids

The original tartan plaids were woven of wool and patterned to designate specific Scottish clans. These patterns have since been popularized far beyond their origins but retain their tribal identities—

Royal Stuart and Gordon are two well-known designs. Like madras checks, these patterns are a mainstay of the campus fashion perpetuated by Ralph Lauren, who uses tartan plaids in everything from underwear to bedsheets. As with

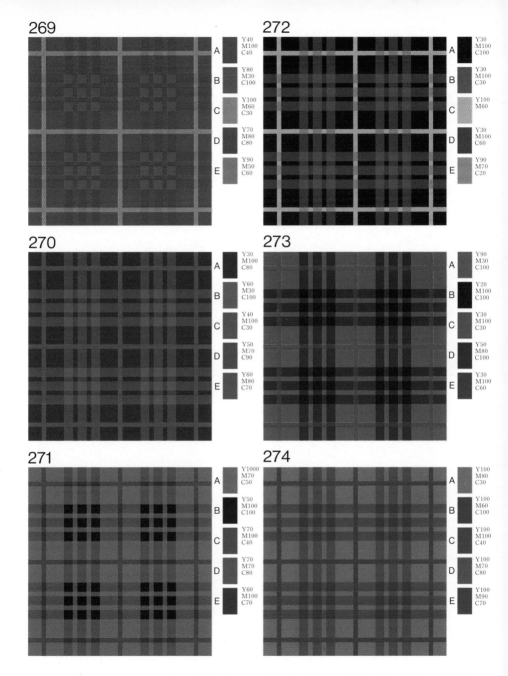

269

A — Y40 M100 C40
B — Y80 M30 C100
C — Y100 M60 C30
D — Y70 M80 C80
E — Y90 M50 C60

272

A — Y30 M100 C100
B — Y30 M100 C30
C — Y100 M60
D — Y30 M100 C60
E — Y90 M70 C20

270

A — Y30 M100 C80
B — Y60 M30 C100
C — Y40 M100 C30
D — Y50 M70 C90
E — Y60 M80 C70

273

A — Y90 M30 C100
B — Y20 M100 C100
C — Y30 M100 C30
D — Y50 M80 C100
E — Y30 M100 C60

271

A — Y1000 M70 C50
B — Y50 M100 C100
C — Y70 M100 C40
D — Y70 M70 C80
E — Y60 M100 C70

274

A — Y100 M80 C30
B — Y100 M60 C100
C — Y100 M100 C40
D — Y100 M70 C80
E — Y100 M90 C70

the other plaids presented in this book, the personalities of individual tartan designs are largely determined by the background color. Examples 263-268 use traditional tartan colors. Examples 269-274, however, freely combine unconven-

tional colors and show how tartan plaids have come to incorporate modern color combinations with no connection to clan patterns.

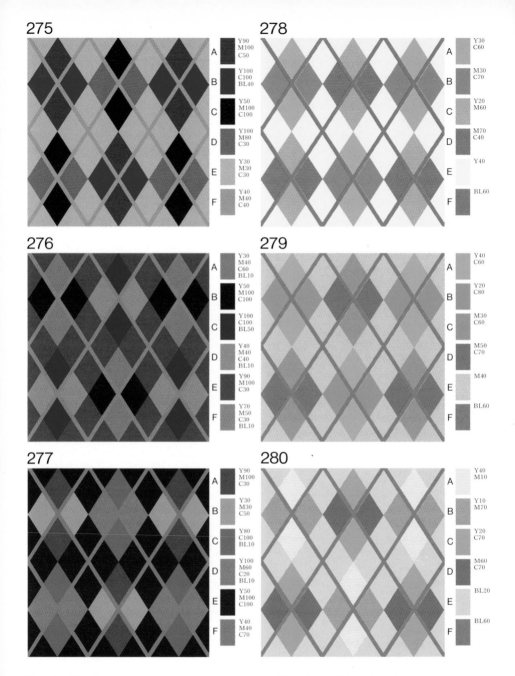

275

A	Y90 M100 C50
B	Y100 C100 BL40
C	Y50 M100 C100
D	Y100 M80 C30
E	Y30 M30 C30
F	Y40 M40 C40

276

A	Y30 M40 C60 BL10
B	Y50 M100 C100
C	Y100 C100 BL50
D	Y40 M40 C40 BL10
E	Y90 M100 C30
F	Y70 M50 C30 BL10

277

A	Y90 M100 C30
B	Y30 M30 C50
C	Y80 C100 BL10
D	Y100 M60 C20 BL10
E	Y50 M100 C100
F	Y40 M40 C70

278

A	Y30 C60
B	M30 C70
C	Y20 M60
D	M70 C40
E	Y40
F	BL60

279

A	Y40 C60
B	Y20 C80
C	M30 C60
D	M50 C70
E	M40
F	BL60

280

A	Y40 M10
B	Y10 M70
C	Y20 C70
D	M60 C70
E	BL20
F	BL60

Argyle Checks

A traditional check pattern named for a branch of the Scottish clan of Campbell, the argyle design consists of diamond shapes defined by thin diagonal lines. The original argyle patterns were col-

ored in subdued, heathered tones of brown and green (examples 284-286). That traditional palette has since been expanded to include the brighter tones shown in examples 275-277. The pastel and neutral color bases with medium-

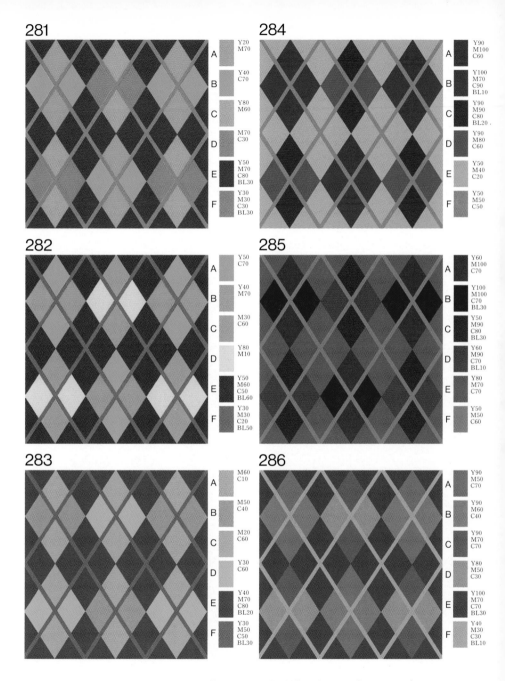

281

A — Y20 M70
B — Y40 C70
C — Y80 M60
D — M70 C30
E — Y50 M70 C80 BL30
F — Y30 M30 C30 BL30

284

A — Y90 M100 C60
B — Y100 M70 C90 BL10
C — Y90 M90 C80 BL20
D — Y90 M80 C60
E — Y50 M40 C20
F — Y50 M50 C50

282

A — Y50 C70
B — Y40 M70
C — M30 C60
D — Y80 M10
E — Y50 M60 C50 BL60
F — Y30 M30 C20 BL50

285

A — Y60 M100 C70
B — Y100 M100 C70 BL30
C — Y50 M90 C80 BL30
D — Y60 M90 C70 BL10
E — Y80 M70 C70
F — Y50 M50 C60

283

A — M60 C10
B — M50 C40
C — M20 C60
D — Y30 C60
E — Y40 M70 C80 BL20
F — Y30 M50 C50 BL30

286

A — Y90 M50 C70
B — Y90 M60 C40
C — Y90 M70 C70
D — Y80 M50 C30
E — Y100 M70 C70 BL30
F — Y40 M30 C30 BL10

bright motifs and dark gray accent lines (examples 278-280), although less conventional, are an interesting color departure that is modern and sophisticated. By introducing an unconventional coloration — the black background in examples

281-283 — the argyle pattern becomes almost unrecognizable and assumes a mosaic quality.

29

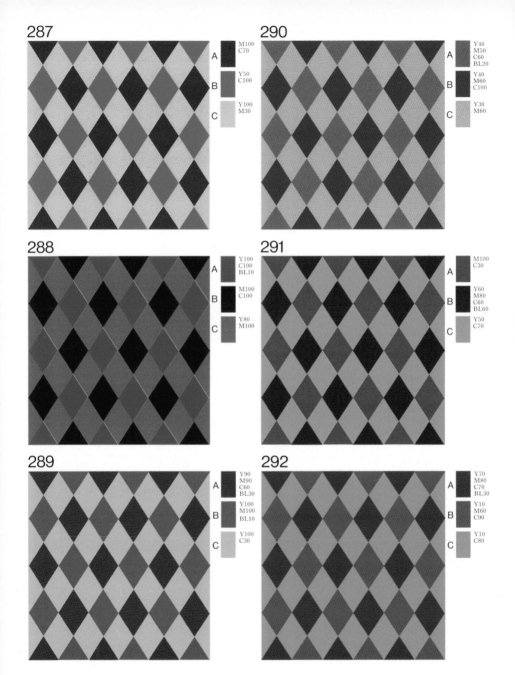

287

A: M100 C70
B: Y50 C100
C: Y100 M30

290

A: Y40 M50 C60 BL20
B: Y40 M60 C100
C: Y30 M60

288

A: Y100 C100 BL10
B: M100 C100
C: Y80 M100

291

A: M100 C30
B: Y60 M80 C60 BL60
C: Y50 C70

289

A: Y90 M90 C60 BL30
B: Y100 M100 BL10
C: Y100 C30

292

A: Y70 M80 C70 BL30
B: Y10 M60 C90
C: Y10 C80

Harlequin Checks

This check design originated in French theater, where the harlequin (a pantomime character) wears a mask, gay spangled tights, and an overshirt printed in a bright, multicolored diamond de-

sign. A variation of the block (*ichimatsu*) design, this simple but powerful pattern is a great attention-getter and very effective on stage. The traditional harlequin brights shown in examples 287-289 cre-

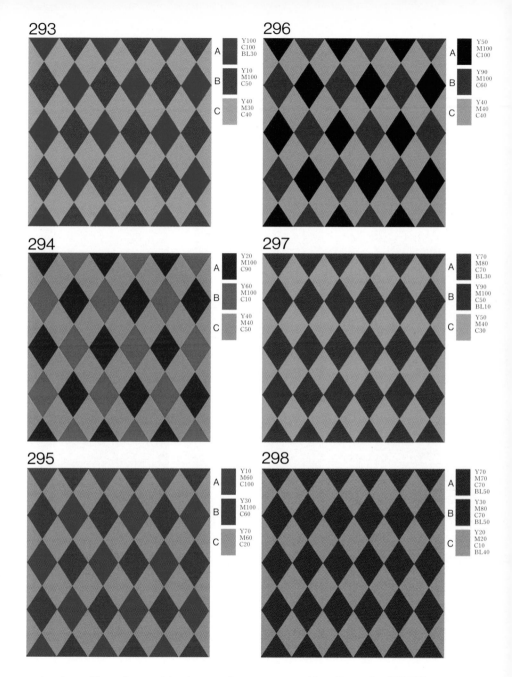

293

A — Y100 C100 BL30
B — Y10 M100 C50
C — Y40 M30 C40

296

A — Y50 M100 C100
B — Y90 M100 C60
C — Y40 M40 C40

294

A — Y20 M100 C90
B — Y60 M100 C10
C — Y40 M40 C50

297

A — Y70 M80 C70 BL30
B — Y90 M100 C50 BL10
C — Y50 M40 C30

295

A — Y10 M60 C100
B — Y30 M100 C60
C — Y70 M60 C20

298

A — Y70 M70 C70 BL50
B — Y30 M80 C70 BL50
C — Y20 M20 C10 BL40

ate circus-like color combinations, and variations of complementary color are used to effect a visual shock. Examples 290-292 use softer base colors and grayed motif colors to quiet the design composition. Examples 293-298 use neutral background colors, and bright motif colors (examples 293-295) are striking against the soft base.

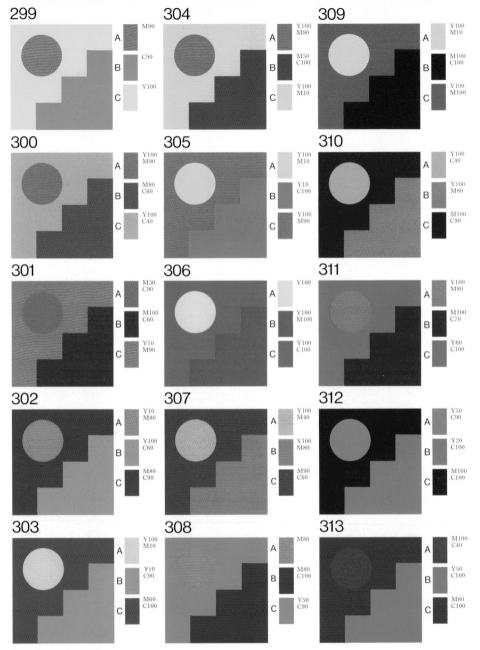

Simple Prints (1)

A successful marriage of composition and color is imperative in creating a design that works. The examples on this page combine a strong, graphic pattern and equally powerful colors to create a striking design. When combined, com-plementary (opposite) colors (red and green in example 306, green and violet in example 300) excite the eye. Placed next to green, red is at its reddest.

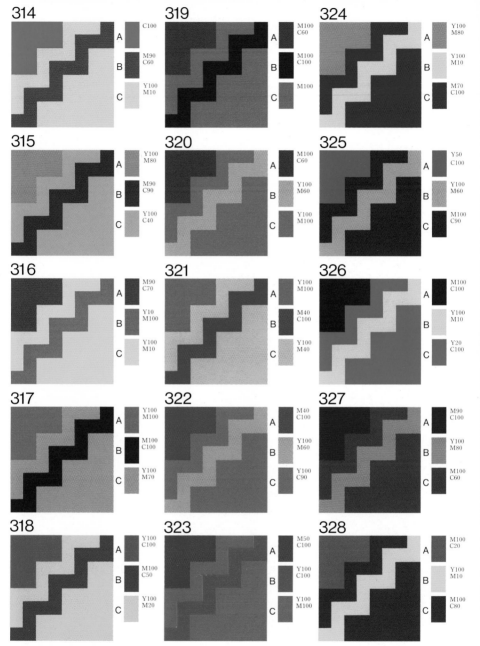

314
A: C100
B: M90 C60
C: Y100 M10

319
A: M100 C60
B: M100 C100
C: M100

324
A: Y100 M80
B: Y100 M10
C: M70 C100

315
A: Y100 M80
B: M90 C90
C: Y100 C40

320
A: M100 C60
B: Y100 M60
C: Y100 M100

325
A: Y50 C100
B: Y100 M60
C: M100 C90

316
A: M90 C70
B: Y10 M100
C: Y100 M10

321
A: Y100 M100
B: M40 C100
C: Y100 M40

326
A: M100 C100
B: Y100 M10
C: Y20 C100

317
A: Y100 M100
B: M100 C100
C: Y100 M70

322
A: M40 C100
B: Y100 M60
C: Y100 C90

327
A: M90 C100
B: Y100 M80
C: M100 C60

318
A: Y100 C100
B: M100 C50
C: Y100 M20

323
A: M50 C100
B: Y100 C100
C: Y100 M100

328
A: M100 C20
B: Y100 M10
C: M100 C80

Simple Prints (2)

Bright chromatic colors, combined with a simple ziggurat (or stair-step) design, create a composition with the same graphic strength as the previous examples. Again, color placement can significantly affect the way the design is perceived. The violet zigzag in example 318, for instance, seems narrower than the orange zigzag in example 325 — they are, in fact, identical in size.

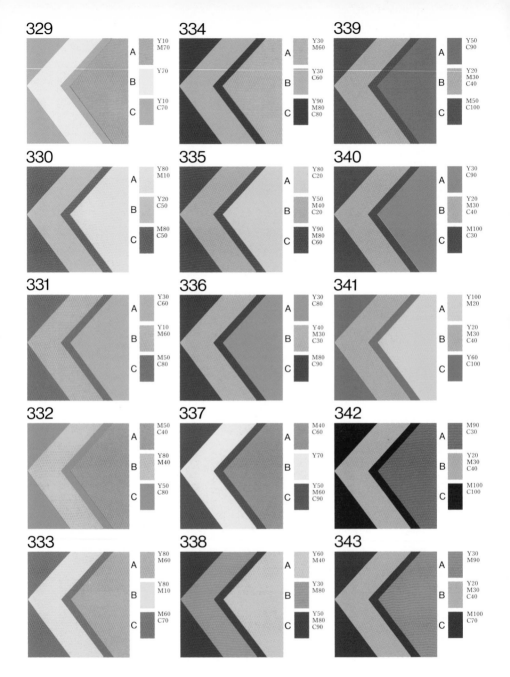

Simple Prints (3)

This design, a variation of the zigzag, is similar in composition to the previous two patterns but uses colors with more subtlety and sophistication. Replacing a chromatic bright with a dusty lilac (example 332), for instance, softens the overall effect considerably. Also, where examples 299-328 produced an unbridled color splurge, examples 339-343 introduce a wide silver-gray stripe to create a controlled, authoritative image.

34

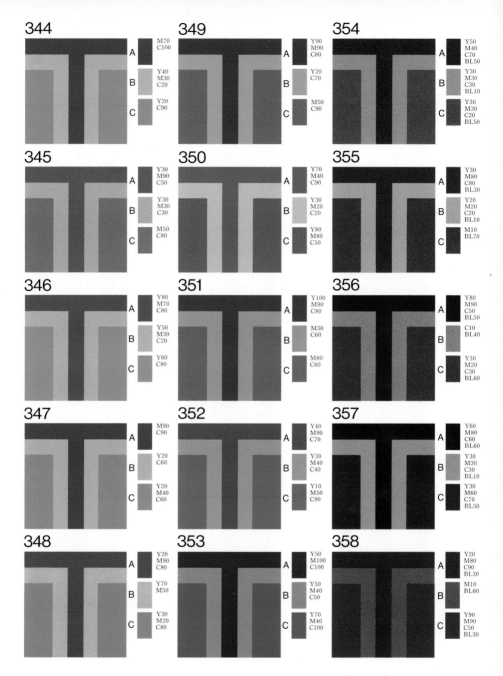

344		345		346	
A	M70 C100	A	Y30 M90 C50	A	Y80 M70 C80
B	Y40 M30 C20	B	Y30 M30 C30	B	Y50 M30 C20
C	Y20 C90	C	M50 C80	C	Y60 C80

349		350		351	
A	Y90 M90 C80	A	Y70 M40 C90	A	Y100 M90 C80
B	Y20 C70	B	Y30 M20 C20	B	M30 C60
C	M50 C90	C	Y80 M80 C50	C	M80 C60

354		355		356	
A	Y50 M40 C70 BL50	A	Y30 M80 C80 BL30	A	Y80 M90 C50 BL50
B	Y30 M30 C30 BL10	B	Y20 M20 C20 BL10	B	C10 BL40
C	Y30 M30 C20 BL50	C	M10 BL70	C	Y30 M20 C30 BL60

347		352		357	
A	M90 C90	A	Y40 M90 C70	A	Y60 M80 C60 BL60
B	Y20 C60	B	Y30 M40 C40	B	Y30 M30 C30 BL10
C	Y20 M40 C60	C	Y10 M50 C90	C	Y30 M60 C70 BL50

348		353		358	
A	Y20 M90 C80	A	Y50 M100 C100	A	Y20 M80 C90 BL30
B	Y70 M50	B	Y50 M40 C50	B	M10 BL60
C	Y30 M20 C80	C	Y70 M40 C100	C	Y90 M90 C50 BL30

Simple Prints (4)

Examples 344-358 show again how color and composition can complement one another. Sober, subdued colors frame the stable T-shaped design, emphasizing the T-shape and projecting a solid, serious image. Most of these colors contain a percentage of gray, which can subdue or reconcile violently contrasting colors. For this reason, a quietly intense saturated color is often referred to as *grayed*.

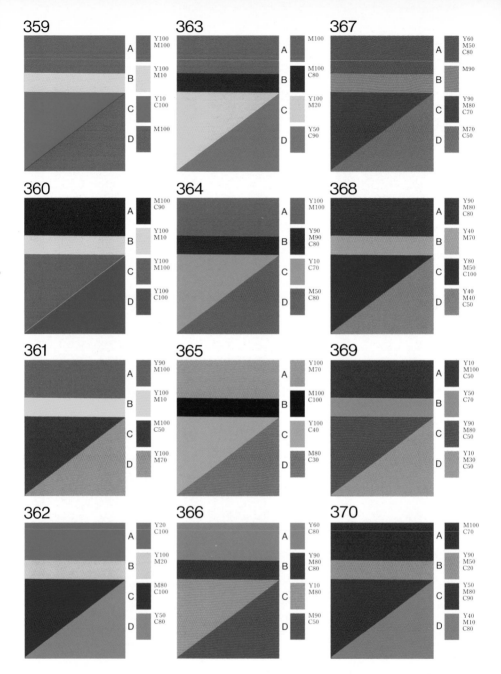

359
A — Y100 M100
B — Y100 M10
C — Y10 C100
D — M100

363
A — M100
B — M100 C80
C — Y100 M20
D — Y50 C90

367
A — Y60 M50 C80
B — M90
C — Y90 M80 C70
D — M70 C50

360
A — M100 C90
B — Y100 M10
C — Y100 M100
D — Y100 C100

364
A — Y100 M100
B — Y90 M90 C80
C — Y10 C70
D — M50 C80

368
A — Y90 M80 C80
B — Y40 M70
C — Y80 M50 C100
D — Y40 M40 C50

361
A — Y90 M100
B — Y100 M10
C — M100 C50
D — Y100 M70

365
A — Y100 M70
B — M100 C100
C — Y100 C40
D — M80 C30

369
A — Y10 M100 C50
B — Y50 C70
C — Y90 M80 C50
D — Y10 M30 C50

362
A — Y20 C100
B — Y100 M20
C — M80 C100
D — Y50 C80

366
A — Y60 C80
B — Y90 M80 C80
C — Y10 M80
D — M90 C50

370
A — M100 C70
B — Y90 M50 C20
C — Y50 M80 C90
D — Y40 M10 C80

Simple Prints (5)

This pattern, created by intersecting lines of color, is the first of these prints to use four colors. The use of those colors makes the design simple and powerful at the same time. The B color, the key to the design, unites the two parts of the composition, while the diagonal line produces a visual tension that breaks the monotony of the top two stripes.

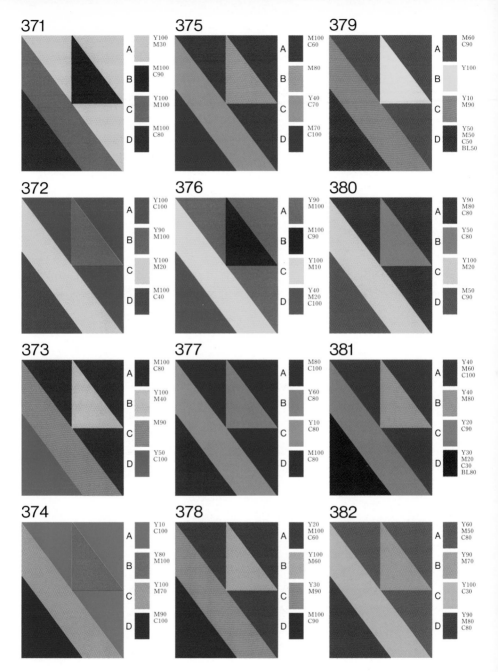

371
A Y100 M30
B M100 C90
C Y100 M100
D M100 C80

375
A M100 C60
B M80
C Y40 C70
D M70 C100

379
A M60 C90
B Y100
C Y10 M90
D Y50 M50 C50 BL50

372
A Y100 C100
B Y90 M100
C Y100 M20
D M100 C40

376
A Y90 M100
B M100 C90
C Y100 M10
D Y40 M20 C100

380
A Y90 M80 C80
B Y50 C80
C Y100 M20
D M50 C90

373
A M100 C80
B Y100 M40
C M90
D Y50 C100

377
A M80 C100
B Y60 C80
C Y10 C80
D M100 C80

381
A Y40 M60 C100
B Y40 M80
C Y20 C90
D Y30 M20 C30 BL80

374
A Y10 C100
B Y80 M100
C Y100 M70
D M90 C100

378
A Y20 M100 C60
B Y100 M60
C Y30 M90
D M100 C90

382
A Y60 M50 C80
B Y90 M70
C Y100 C30
D Y90 M80 C80

Simple Prints (6)

The triangle is the key to this sharply patterned design. The free use of intersecting lines gives each example a geometric personality that is energized by the precarious placement of the triangle on the diagonal. The bright, vivid triangle colors in examples 371-374 are complementary (or nearly so) to the base colors. Unusual darks and deep blues (examples 379-382) introduce unexpected color jolts.

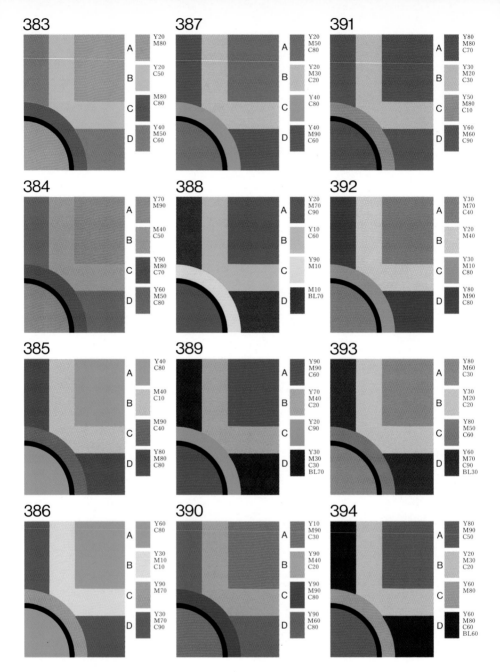

Simple Prints (7)

This sleek, modern design seems to use many more colors than the previous design — in fact, each example uses just four colors (and black). The visual deception occurs because one color ap-

pears twice — the center of the square and the center of the circle — and because a thin black line is used to make the circle color appear stronger and more vivid than the square color.

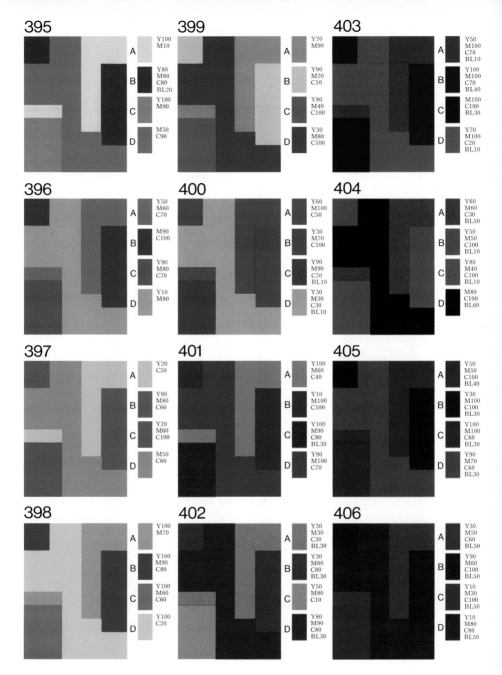

395

A — Y100 M10
B — Y80 M80 C80 BL20
C — Y100 M90
D — M50 C90

399

A — Y70 M90
B — Y90 M20 C10
C — Y80 M40 C100
D — Y30 M80 C100

403

A — Y50 M100 C70 BL10
B — Y100 M100 C70 BL40
C — M100 C100 BL30
D — Y70 M100 C20 BL10

396

A — Y50 M60 C70
B — M90 C100
C — Y90 M80 C70
D — Y10 M80

400

A — Y60 M100 C50
B — Y30 M70 C100
C — Y90 M90 C70 BL10
D — Y30 M30 C30 BL10

404

A — Y60 M60 C30 BL50
B — Y50 M50 C100 BL10
C — Y80 M40 C100 BL10
D — M80 C100 BL60

397

A — Y20 C50
B — Y90 M80 C60
C — Y20 M60 C100
D — M50 C60

401

A — Y100 M60 C40
B — Y10 M100 C100
C — Y100 M90 C80 BL30
D — Y90 M100 C70

405

A — Y50 M50 C100 BL40
B — Y30 M100 C100 BL30
C — Y100 M100 C60 BL30
D — Y90 M70 C60 BL30

398

A — Y100 M70
B — Y100 M90 C80
C — Y100 M60 C60
D — Y100 C20

402

A — Y30 M30 C30 BL30
B — Y30 M80 C80 BL30
C — Y50 M80 C10
D — Y80 M90 C80 BL30

406

A — Y30 M50 C60 BL50
B — Y90 M60 C100 BL50
C — Y10 M30 C100 BL50
D — Y10 M80 C80 BL50

Simple Prints (8)

This two-dimensional block pattern repeats the A and B colors in each example, but the absence of a black accent flattens the design and makes it less interesting than the last. Again, color controls the personality of the composition — the primary and charcoal mix in example 395 is Mondrian-like, while examples 400-402 are reminiscent of combinations popular in the fifties.

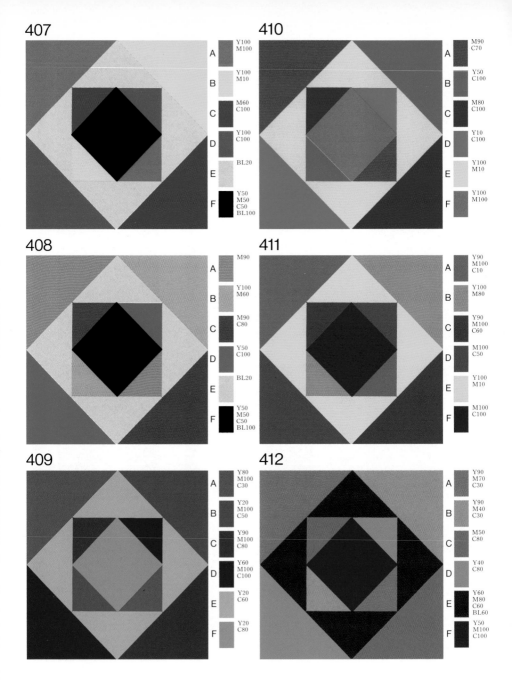

Simple Prints (9)

The rose pattern, an example of geometric abstraction, is formed by a series of squares. From the perimeter, the square is repeated—first on the straight, then on the diagonal—until the last square

creates the center of the rose. This design uses six colors, repeating the colors of the outer triangles in the center triangles, and can be used effectively to test color relationships.

40

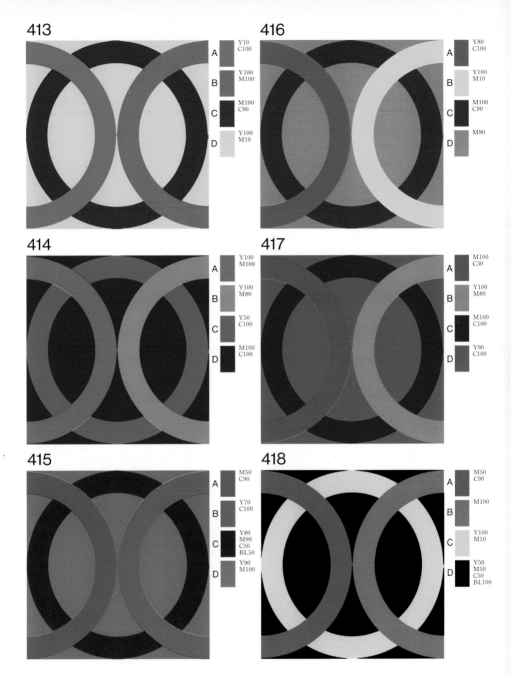

413

A	Y10 C100
B	Y100 M100
C	M100 C90
D	Y100 M10

416

A	Y80 C100
B	Y100 M10
C	M100 C90
D	M90

414

A	Y100 M100
B	Y100 M80
C	Y50 C100
D	M100 C100

417

A	M100 C30
B	Y100 M80
C	M100 C100
D	Y90 C100

415

A	M50 C90
B	Y70 C100
C	Y80 M90 C50 BL50
D	Y90 M100

418

A	M50 C90
B	M100
C	Y100 M10
D	Y50 M50 C50 BL100

Simple Prints (10)

Suggestive of the Olympic logo (symbol), this bold graphic derives its strength from its simplicity and is most effective in brilliant chromatics that visually balance the bigness of the design. Examples 413 and 418 are particularly dramatic because of the yellow and black backgrounds. Since black represents maximum darkness, the brights "pop" forward with even more energy than usual.

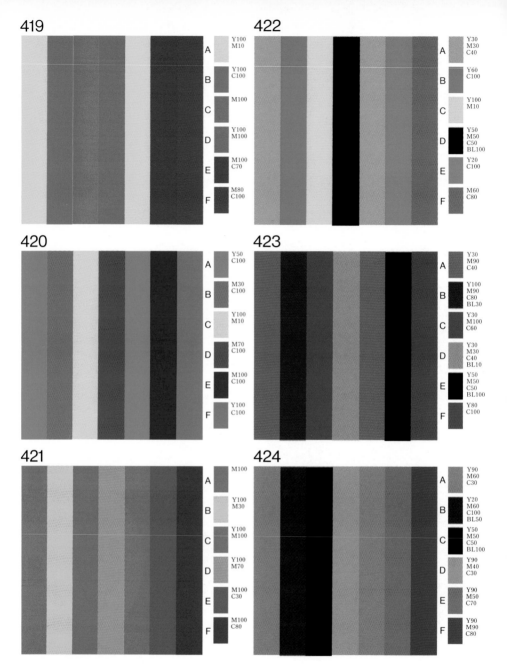

419

A	Y100 M10
B	Y100 C100
C	M100
D	Y100 M100
E	M100 C70
F	M80 C100

422

A	Y30 M30 C40
B	Y60 C100
C	Y100 M10
D	Y50 M50 C50 BL100
E	Y20 C100
F	M60 C80

420

A	Y50 C100
B	M30 C100
C	Y100 M10
D	M70 C100
E	M100 C100
F	Y100 C100

423

A	Y30 M90 C40
B	Y100 M90 C80 BL30
C	Y30 M100 C60
D	Y30 M30 C40 BL10
E	Y50 M50 C50 BL100
F	Y80 C100

421

A	M100
B	Y100 M30
C	Y100 M100
D	Y100 M70
E	M100 C30
F	M100 C80

424

A	Y90 M60 C30
B	Y20 M60 C100 BL50
C	Y50 M50 C50 BL100
D	Y90 M40 C30
E	Y90 M50 C70
F	Y90 M90 C80

Simple Prints (11)

The variously colored stripes in examples 419-430 create diverse color impressions. In the randomly positioned bright color ribbons in examples 419-421, the A color is repeated to control and emphasize the tone. Although yellow dominates example 422, the gray stripes calm the composition, and the black stripe adds a dramatic tension to create

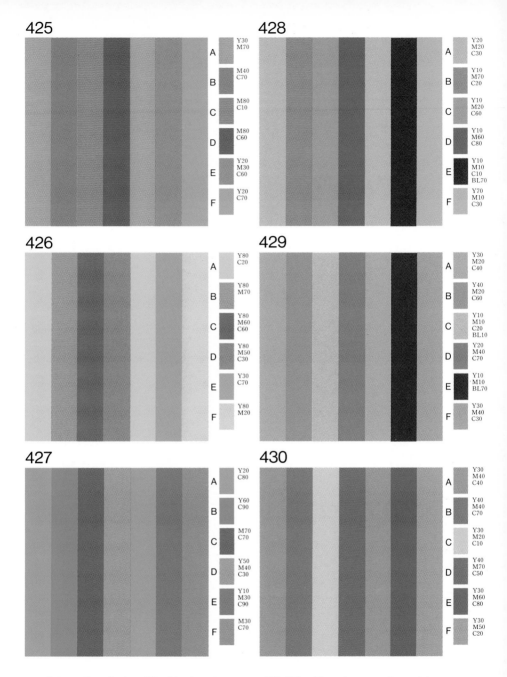

425

A	Y30 M70
B	M40 C70
C	M80 C10
D	M80 C60
E	Y20 M30 C60
F	Y20 C70

428

A	Y20 M20 C30
B	Y10 M70 C20
C	Y10 M20 C60
D	Y10 M60 C80
E	Y10 M10 C10 BL70
F	Y70 M10 C30

426

A	Y80 C20
B	Y80 M70
C	Y80 M60 C60
D	Y80 M50 C30
E	Y30 C70
F	Y80 M20

429

A	Y30 M20 C40
B	Y40 M20 C60
C	Y10 M10 C20 BL10
D	Y20 M40 C70
E	Y10 M10 BL70
F	Y30 M40 C30

427

A	Y20 C80
B	Y60 C90
C	M70 C70
D	Y50 M40 C30
E	Y10 M30 C90
F	M30 C70

430

A	Y30 M40 C40
B	Y40 M40 C70
C	Y30 M20 C10
D	Y40 M70 C50
E	Y30 M60 C80
F	Y30 M50 C20

an interesting design. The black stripes in examples 423-424 show how a small dose of contrasting color can enliven a tonal (same-family) color composition. The medium-to-soft brights in examples 425-428, although unusual, combine easily. The soft, chalky tones in examples 429-430 also mix well and create pleasant, neutral stripings.

43

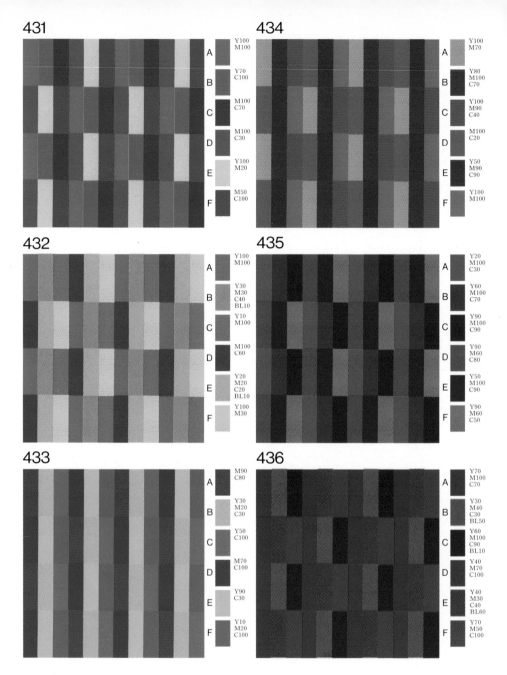

Quilt Patterns (1)

Early American patchwork quilts were made from fabric scraps cut into geometric shapes and worked into traditional patterns. Some quilts required years to complete, but the results were so spectacular that some of these quilts now hang in museums as works of art. Color placement and repetition are very important in the design—as in example 433, where brights and neutrals contrast to create distinct vertical lines.

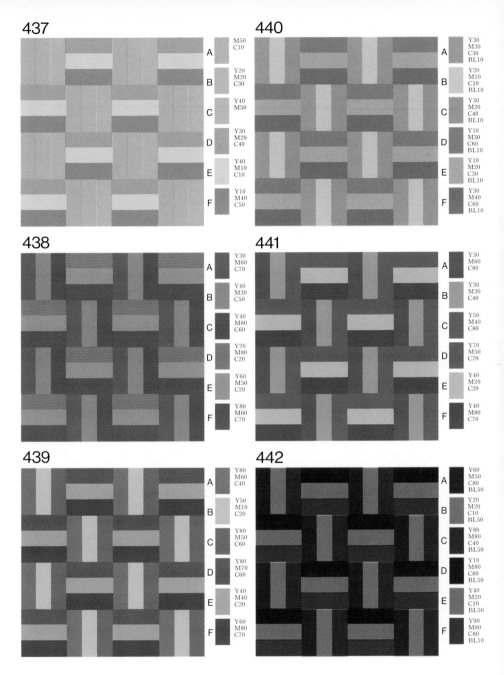

437

A	M50 C10
B	Y20 M20 C30
C	Y40 M50
D	Y30 M20 C40
E	Y40 M10 C10
F	Y10 M40 C50

440

A	Y30 M30 C30 BL10
B	Y20 M10 C10 BL10
C	Y30 M20 C40 BL10
D	Y10 M30 C60 BL10
E	Y10 M20 C30 BL10
F	Y30 M40 C60 BL10

438

A	Y30 M60 C70
B	Y40 M30 C50
C	Y40 M80 C60
D	Y20 M80 C20
E	Y60 M50 C20
F	Y80 M60 C70

441

A	Y30 M60 C80
B	Y30 M30 C40
C	Y50 M40 C80
D	Y70 M50 C70
E	Y40 M20 C20
F	Y40 M80 C70

439

A	Y80 M60 C40
B	Y50 M10 C20
C	Y80 M50 C60
D	Y80 M70 C60
E	Y40 M40 C20
F	Y60 M80 C70

442

A	Y60 M50 C80 BL50
B	Y20 M20 C10 BL50
C	Y80 M80 C40 BL50
D	Y10 M80 C80 BL50
E	Y40 M20 C10 BL50
F	Y90 M80 C80 BL10

Quilt Patterns (2)

This traditional design uses alternating horizontal and vertical blocks of the same size to create a basketweave appearance. The soft, neutral tones in examples 437-442 result in graphic, aesthetically pleasing combinations. In each example, the careful placement of color — the light central rectangle and the dark base rectangle in the horizontal block — strengthens the design and emphasizes the basketweave theme.

45

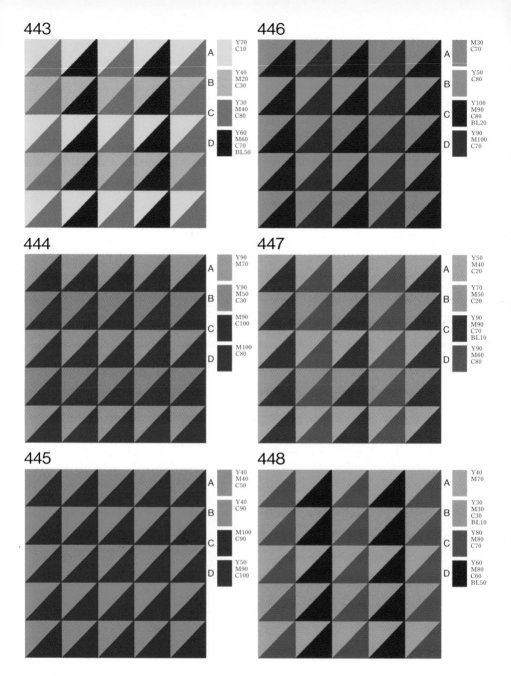

443

A — Y70 C10
B — Y40 M20 C30
C — Y30 M40 C80
D — Y60 M60 C70 BL50

446

A — M30 C70
B — Y50 C80
C — Y100 M90 C80 BL20
D — Y90 M100 C70

444

A — Y90 M70
B — Y90 M50 C30
C — M90 C100
D — M100 C80

447

A — Y50 M40 C20
B — Y70 M50 C20
C — Y90 M90 C70 BL10
D — Y90 M60 C80

445

A — Y40 M40 C50
B — Y40 C90
C — M100 C90
D — Y50 M90 C100

448

A — Y40 M70
B — Y30 M30 C30 BL10
C — Y80 M80 C70
D — Y60 M80 C60 BL50

Quilt Patterns (3)

The triangle-made squares in examples 443-448 stimulate the eye so that the design acquires a kinetic (moving) quality. The use of highly contrasting colors gives this traditional quilting design a contemporary look that rivals op art. Each square has a light and a dark triangle and is divided by a diagonal line, thereby producing optimum contrast and maximum movement.

46

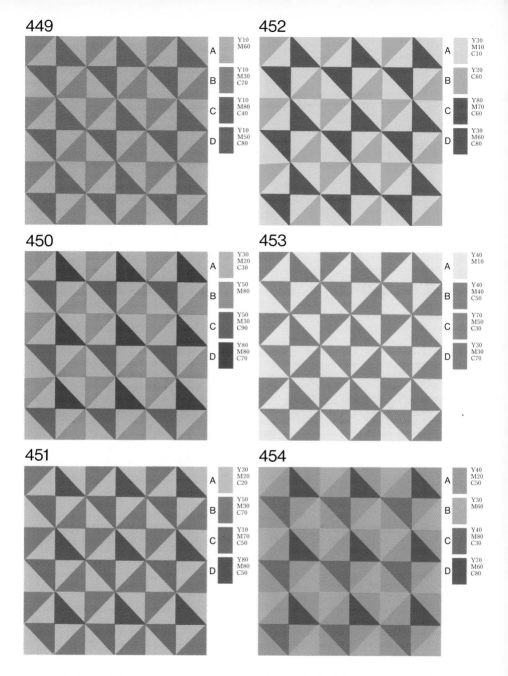

449

A — Y10 M60

B — Y10 M30 C70

C — Y10 M80 C40

D — Y10 M50 C80

452

A — Y30 M10 C10

B — Y20 C60

C — Y80 M70 C60

D — Y30 M60 C80

450

A — Y30 M20 C30

B — Y50 M80

C — Y50 M30 C90

D — Y80 M80 C70

453

A — Y40 M10

B — Y40 M40 C50

C — Y70 M50 C30

D — Y30 M30 C70

451

A — Y30 M20 C20

B — Y50 M30 C70

C — Y10 M70 C50

D — Y80 M80 C50

454

A — Y40 M20 C50

B — Y30 M60

C — Y40 M80 C30

D — Y70 M60 C80

Quilt Patterns (4)

As with the previous pattern, a diagonal line separates the squares in this design. These examples, however, alternate lights and darks to create a playful symmetry that softens the image and produces a lyrical, feminine composition. The medium brights and neutrals used here offer contrast without harshness. The A color is the dominant force in each example, with a ratio of 4:2:1:1.

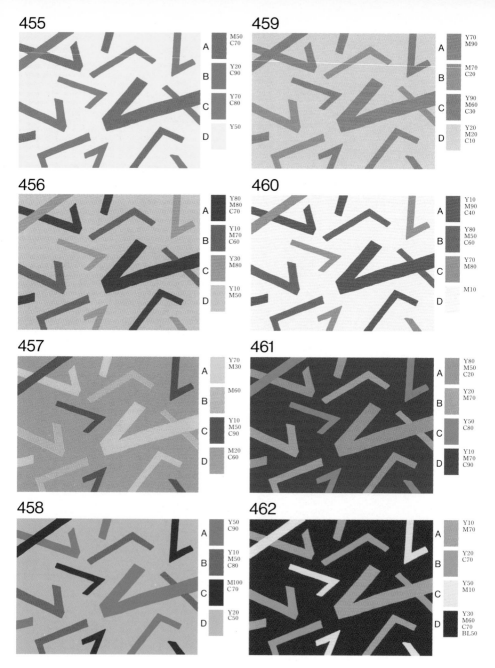

455	A	M50 C70
	B	Y20 C90
	C	Y70 C80
	D	Y50
459	A	Y70 M90
	B	M70 C20
	C	Y90 M60 C30
	D	Y20 M20 C10
456	A	Y80 M80 C70
	B	Y10 M70 C60
	C	Y30 M80
	D	Y10 M50
460	A	Y10 M90 C40
	B	Y80 M50 C60
	C	Y70 M80
	D	M10
457	A	Y70 M30
	B	M60
	C	Y10 M50 C90
	D	M20 C60
461	A	Y80 M50 C20
	B	Y20 M70
	C	Y50 C80
	D	Y10 M70 C90
458	A	Y50 C90
	B	Y10 M50 C80
	C	M100 C70
	D	Y20 C50
462	A	Y10 M70
	B	Y20 C70
	C	Y50 M10
	D	Y30 M60 C70 BL50

Abstract Print Patterns (1)
In the early 20th century, Matisse's paper cutouts were considered scandalously avant-garde. Now, of course, this simple but energetic type of imagery appears in everything from fine art to lunch boxes.

The appeal of these scattered designs — which have a whimsical, almost childlike character — is the freshness and sense of freedom that they project. The colors used strengthen the message.

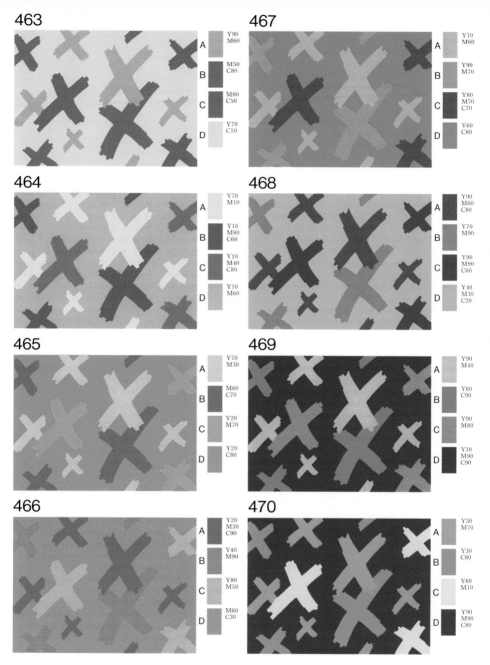

463

A	Y90 M60
B	M50 C80
C	M80 C50
D	Y70 C10

467

A	Y10 M60
B	Y90 M70
C	Y80 M70 C70
D	Y60 C80

464

A	Y70 M10
B	Y10 M80 C60
C	Y10 M40 C80
D	Y10 M60

468

A	Y90 M60 C80
B	Y70 M90
C	Y90 M90 C60
D	Y40 M30 C20

465

A	Y70 M30
B	M60 C70
C	Y20 M70
D	Y20 C80

469

A	Y90 M40
B	Y60 C90
C	Y90 M80
D	Y10 M90 C90

466

A	Y20 M30 C90
B	Y40 M90
C	Y80 M50
D	M60 C30

470

A	Y30 M70
B	Y30 C80
C	Y60 M10
D	Y90 M90 C80

Abstract Print Patterns (2)

The free-form crosses floating across this design have an unfinished quality, as if they were still in the process of being painted. The bright, acrid color combinations—such as the startling and un- conventional mixes in examples 463-467 —support the graffiti-like feeling and contribute to the impulsive, punk look. The colors in examples 468-470 are just as strong but far more conventional.

49

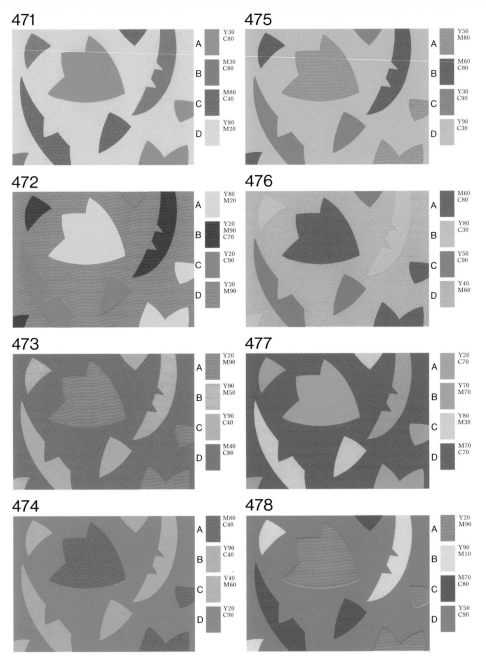

471

A	Y30 C80
B	M30 C80
C	M80 C40
D	Y80 M20

475

A	Y50 M80
B	M60 C80
C	Y30 C90
D	Y90 C30

472

A	Y80 M20
B	Y20 M90 C70
C	Y20 C90
D	Y30 M90

476

A	M60 C80
B	Y80 C30
C	Y50 C90
D	Y40 M60

473

A	Y20 M90
B	Y90 M50
C	Y90 C40
D	M40 C80

477

A	Y20 C70
B	Y70 M70
C	Y80 M30
D	M70 C70

474

A	M80 C40
B	Y90 C40
C	Y40 M60
D	Y20 C90

478

A	Y20 M90
B	Y90 M10
C	M70 C80
D	Y50 C90

Abstract Print Patterns (3)

Even though the flower motif is abstracted in this Matisse-inspired design — cutouts scattered on a colored background — the composition as a whole is representational and creates a light-hearted, feminine pattern. The D (background) color is of primary importance because of the open spacing of the design. The A color, which appears in the flower motif, is the second color priority.

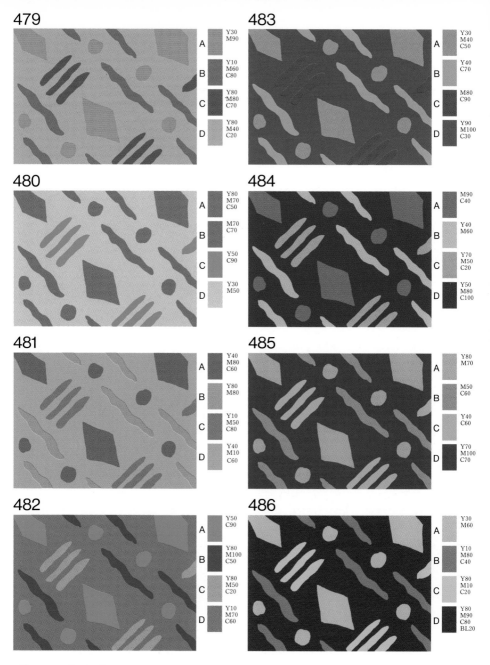

479

A: Y30 M90
B: Y10 M60 C80
C: Y80 M80 C70
D: Y80 M40 C20

483

A: Y30 M40 C50
B: Y40 C70
C: M80 C90
D: Y90 M100 C30

480

A: Y80 M70 C50
B: M70 C70
C: Y50 C90
D: Y30 M50

484

A: M90 C40
B: Y40 M60
C: Y70 M50 C20
D: Y50 M80 C100

481

A: Y40 M80 C60
B: Y80 M80
C: Y10 M50 C80
D: Y40 M10 C60

485

A: Y80 M70
B: M50 C60
C: Y40 C60
D: Y70 M100 C70

482

A: Y50 C90
B: Y80 M100 C50
C: Y80 M50 C20
D: Y10 M70 C60

486

A: Y30 M60
B: Y10 M80 C40
C: Y80 M10 C20
D: Y80 M90 C80 BL20

Abstract Print Patterns (4)

The diagonal stripe design in examples 479-486 borrows ideas from previous print patterns yet projects a unique character. The freely drawn motifs and the regularity of this almost traditional de- sign unexpectedly produce a provocative pattern. The open expanse of background again emphasizes the D (background) color; the overall color feeling, controlled by the A color, is excitingly innovative.

51

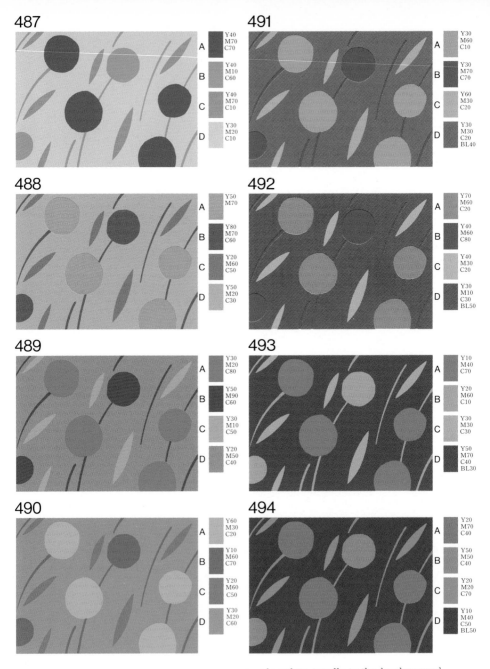

487

A	Y40 M70 C70
B	Y40 M10 C60
C	Y40 M70 C10
D	Y30 M20 C10

491

A	Y30 M60 C10
B	Y30 M70 C70
C	Y60 M30 C20
D	Y30 M30 C20 BL40

488

A	Y50 M70
B	Y80 M70 C60
C	Y20 M60 C50
D	Y50 M20 C30

492

A	Y70 M60 C20
B	Y40 M60 C80
C	Y40 M30 C20
D	Y30 M10 C30 BL50

489

A	Y30 M20 C80
B	Y50 M90 C60
C	Y30 M10 C50
D	Y20 M50 C40

493

A	Y10 M40 C70
B	Y20 M60 C10
C	Y30 M30 C30
D	Y50 M70 C40 BL30

490

A	Y60 M30 C20
B	Y10 M60 C70
C	Y20 M60 C50
D	Y30 M20 C60

494

A	Y20 M70 C40
B	Y50 M50 C40
C	Y20 M20 C70
D	Y10 M40 C50 BL50

Abstract Print Patterns (5)

This abstract floral pattern has a dreamy quality enhanced by color selection. From example 487 to 494, the tone of the background color graduates from beige to charcoal. The motif colors in each ex-

ample relate tonally to the background to create a soft harmony. When medium brights and chalky lights are used for the B color, which contrasts with the base color, the design acquires dimension.

52

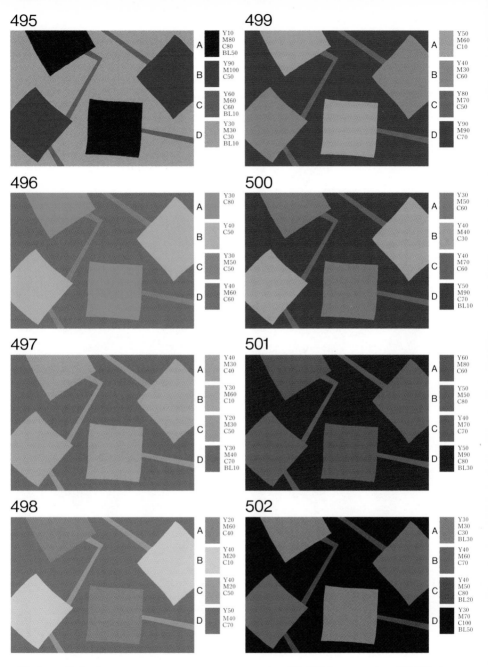

495

A Y10 M80 C80 BL50
B Y90 M100 C50
C Y60 M60 C60 BL10
D Y30 M30 C30 BL10

496

A Y30 C80
B Y40 C50
C Y30 M50 C50
D Y40 M60 C60

497

A Y40 M30 C40
B Y30 M60 C10
C Y20 M30 C50
D Y30 M40 C70 BL10

498

A Y20 M60 C40
B Y40 M20 C10
C Y40 M20 C50
D Y50 M40 C70

499

A Y50 M60 C10
B Y40 M30 C60
C Y80 M70 C50
D Y90 M90 C70

500

A Y30 M50 C60
B Y40 M40 C30
C Y40 M70 C60
D Y50 M90 C70 BL10

501

A Y60 M80 C60
B Y50 M50 C80
C Y40 M70 C70
D Y50 M90 C80 BL30

502

A Y30 M30 C30 BL30
B Y40 M60 C70
C Y40 M50 C80 BL20
D Y30 M70 C100 BL50

Abstract Print Patterns (6)

Although it has its origins in the "cutout school," this design differs greatly from the Matisse-like floral design on page 50. The colors used here are direct opposites of the brightly colored prints in examples 471-478. In examples 495-502, the background colors range from grayed pastels to soft, dusty darks, and the motif colors are appropriately subtle and sophisticated.

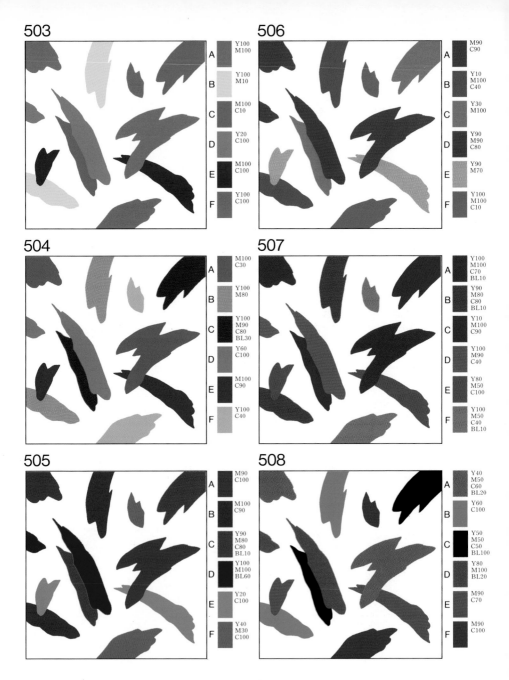

503

A	Y100 M100
B	Y100 M10
C	M100 C10
D	Y20 C100
E	M100 C100
F	Y100 C100

506

A	M90 C90
B	Y10 M100 C40
C	Y30 M100
D	Y90 M90 C80
E	Y90 M70
F	Y100 M100 C10

504

A	M100 C30
B	Y100 M80
C	Y100 M90 C80 BL30
D	Y60 C100
E	M100 C90
F	Y100 C40

507

A	Y100 M100 C70 BL10
B	Y90 M80 C80 BL10
C	Y10 M100 C90
D	Y100 M90 C40
E	Y80 M50 C100
F	Y100 M50 C40 BL10

505

A	M90 C100
B	M100 C90
C	Y90 M80 C80 BL10
D	Y100 M100 BL60
E	Y20 C100
F	Y40 M30 C100

508

A	Y40 M50 C60 BL20
B	Y60 C100
C	Y50 M50 C50 BL100
D	Y80 M100 BL20
E	M90 C70
F	M90 C100

Painting Pattern

This carefree, splatter-cloth print is a popular version of what began as abstract expressionist art. The random splotches of color seem accidental and, therefore, exuberant and free in spirit.

54

The stark white background supports the simple, modern personality of the design and dominates the composition, creating similar color impressions in the examples even though various color motifs are used.

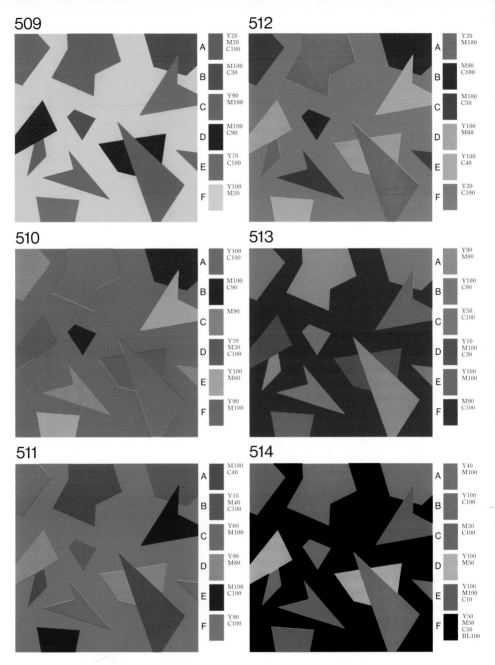

509

A	Y20 M20 C100
B	M100 C30
C	Y90 M100
D	M100 C90
E	Y70 C100
F	Y100 M20

512

A	Y20 M100
B	M90 C100
C	M100 C50
D	Y100 M60
E	Y100 C40
F	Y20 C100

510

A	Y100 C100
B	M100 C90
C	M90
D	Y20 M30 C100
E	Y100 M60
F	Y90 M100

513

A	Y90 M80
B	Y100 C90
C	Y50 C100
D	Y10 M100 C30
E	Y100 M100
F	M90 C100

511

A	M100 C40
B	Y10 M40 C100
C	Y60 M100
D	Y90 M80
E	M100 C100
F	Y90 C100

514

A	Y40 M100
B	Y100 C100
C	M30 C100
D	Y100 M50
E	Y100 M100 C10
F	Y50 M50 C50 BL100

Paper-Cut Pattern

This fresh, appealing pattern looks as if it were made from the haphazard cutting of brightly colored paper. The charm of the design is in the spontaneity of the motif colors and shapes. The seemingly random flurry of intersecting primary color is kept in check by the background color. The simplicity of the design lends itself to any color range, but the brights convey a strong visual message very well.

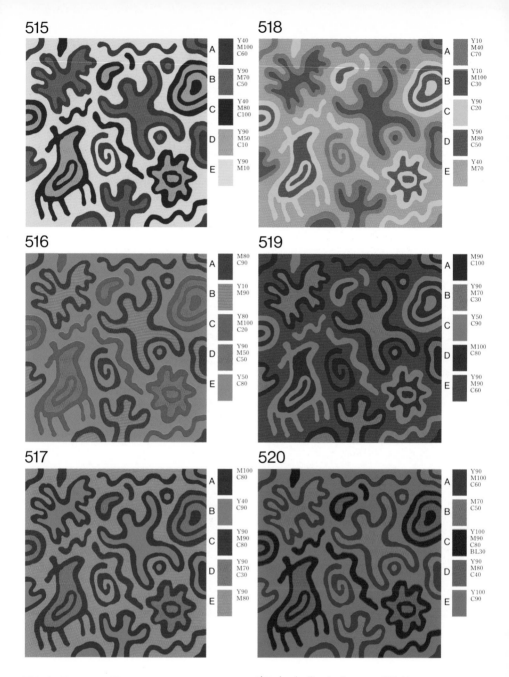

515

A — Y40 M100 C60
B — Y90 M70 C50
C — Y40 M80 C100
D — Y90 M50 C10
E — Y90 M10

518

A — Y10 M40 C70
B — Y10 M100 C30
C — Y90 C20
D — Y90 M80 C50
E — Y40 M70

516

A — M80 C90
B — Y10 M90
C — Y80 M100 C20
D — Y90 M50 C50
E — Y50 C80

519

A — M90 C100
B — Y90 M70 C30
C — Y50 C90
D — M100 C80
E — Y90 M90 C60

517

A — M100 C80
B — Y40 C90
C — Y90 M90 C80
D — Y90 M70 C30
E — Y90 M80

520

A — Y90 M100 C60
B — M70 C50
C — Y100 M90 C80 BL30
D — Y90 M80 C40
E — Y100 C90

Ethnic Patterns (1)

This whimsical interpretation of a primitive cave painting takes ancient motifs and makes them new with color and free-form shapes. Delightfully energetic in both composition and color, this design is similar to the art of Keith Haring. The iconoclastic color combinations used in examples 515-520 are the perfect vehicles for the evocative imagery.

56

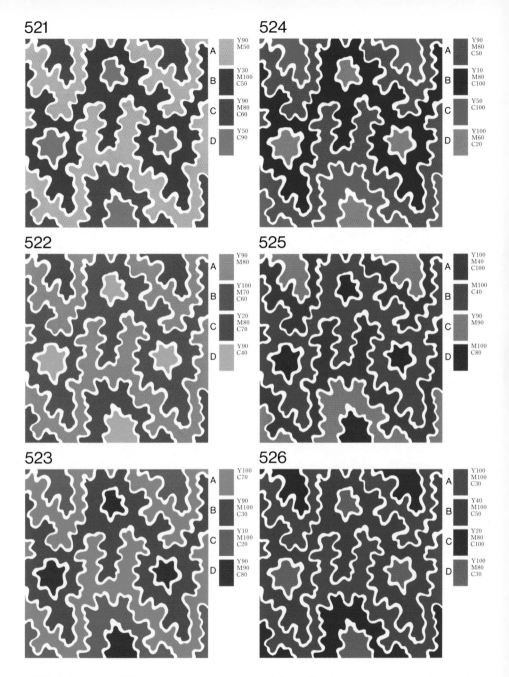

521

A	Y90 M50
B	Y30 M100 C50
C	Y90 M80 C60
D	Y50 C90

524

A	Y90 M80 C50
B	Y10 M80 C100
C	Y50 C100
D	Y100 M60 C20

522

A	Y90 M80
B	Y100 M70 C60
C	Y20 M80 C70
D	Y90 C40

525

A	Y100 M40 C100
B	M100 C40
C	Y90 M90
D	M100 C80

523

A	Y100 C70
B	Y90 M100 C30
C	Y10 M100 C20
D	Y90 M90 C80

526

A	Y100 M100 C30
B	Y40 M100 C50
C	Y20 M80 C100
D	Y100 M80 C30

Ethnic Patterns (2)

Although related to batik, this kinetic color composition is considered abstract because of the flat image of the design and colors. The examples have no distinguishable background color, but the white outline keeps the pattern clear and the colors bright. The brights mixed with earth colors produce a tropical feeling typical of an ethnic color palette. This pattern could be overwhelming in large doses.

57

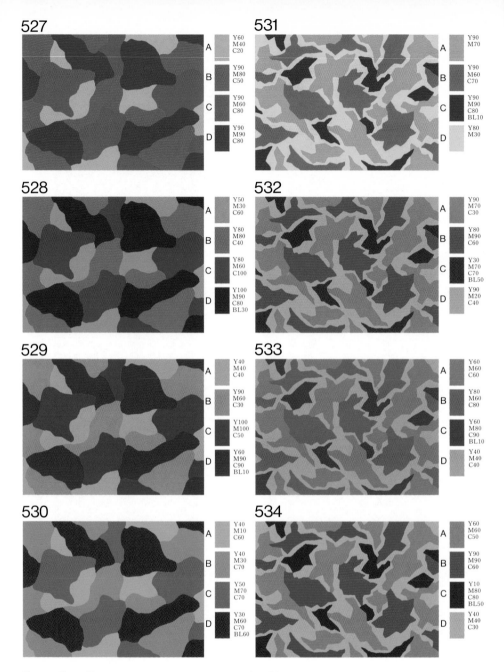

527

A — Y60 M40 C20
B — Y90 M80 C50
C — Y90 M60 C80
D — Y90 M90 C80

528

A — Y50 M30 C60
B — Y80 M80 C40
C — Y80 M60 C100
D — Y100 M90 C80 BL30

529

A — Y40 M40 C40
B — Y90 M60 C30
C — Y100 M100 C50
D — Y60 M90 C90 BL10

530

A — Y40 M10 C60
B — Y40 M30 C70
C — Y50 M70 C70
D — Y30 M60 C70 BL60

531

A — Y90 M70
B — Y90 M60 C70
C — Y90 M90 C80 BL10
D — Y80 M30

532

A — Y90 M70 C30
B — Y80 M90 C60
C — Y30 M70 C70 BL50
D — Y90 M20 C40

533

A — Y60 M60 C60
B — Y80 M60 C80
C — Y60 M80 C90 BL10
D — Y40 M40 C40

534

A — Y60 M60 C50
B — Y90 M90 C60
C — Y10 M80 C80 BL50
D — Y40 M40 C30

Camouflage Pattern

Camouflage is a pattern traditionally used to make military uniforms that blend with the environment and are un-detectable by the enemy. Earth tones (example 527), the original colors used

for this pattern, are still the most popular. Lately, however, the design has become fashionable and makes use of various color combinations (examples 529-530). A variation of the pattern is shown in ex-amples 531-534, where all the naturally

58

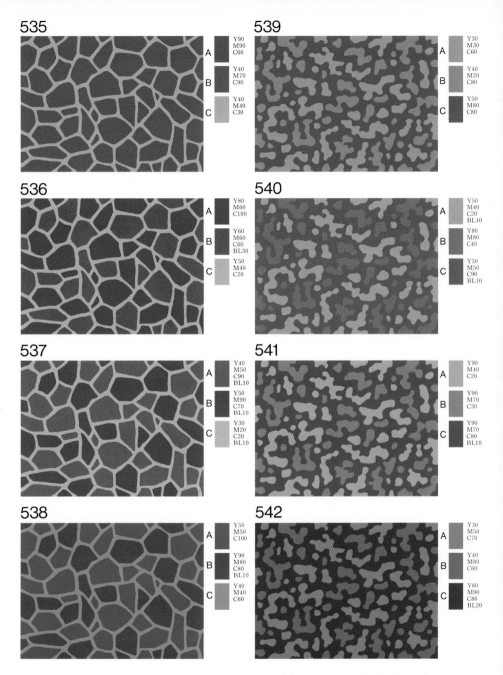

535

A	Y90 M90 C60
B	Y40 M70 C90
C	Y40 M40 C30

536

A	Y80 M60 C100
B	Y60 M60 C60 BL30
C	Y50 M40 C20

537

A	Y40 M50 C90 BL10
B	Y50 M90 C70 BL10
C	Y30 M20 C20 BL10

538

A	Y50 M50 C100
B	Y90 M80 C80 BL10
C	Y40 M40 C60

539

A	Y30 M30 C60
B	Y40 M20 C80
C	Y50 M80 C80

540

A	Y50 M40 C20 BL10
B	Y80 M80 C40
C	Y50 M50 C90 BL10

541

A	Y90 M40 C20
B	Y90 M70 C30
C	Y90 M70 C80 BL10

542

A	Y30 M50 C70
B	Y40 M80 C60
C	Y80 M90 C80 BL20

occurring colors are related. Examples 535-538 show another camouflage variation that resembles cracked mud because of the natural colors used. If the outlines were black and the motifs brightly colored, the design would re-

semble abstract stained glass. The design in examples 539-542 is small but reflective, like light off of water.

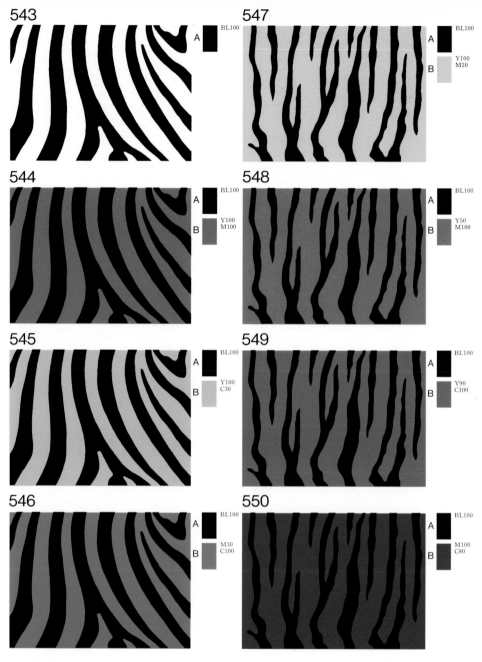

543
A — BL100

547
A — BL100
B — Y100 M20

544
A — BL100
B — Y100 M100

548
A — BL100
B — Y50 M100

545
A — BL100
B — Y100 C30

549
A — BL100
B — Y90 C100

546
A — BL100
B — M30 C100

550
A — BL100
B — M100 C80

Animal Pattern

In the past twenty years, animal patterns have become a major fashion trend and such an important design motif that they are grouped, like florals and abstracts, in a class by themselves. These pages con-

tain four modern and graphic animal prints — zebra, tiger, giraffe, and leopard. The first example in each set (543, 547, 551, and 555) is colored naturally — the zebra is black and white, the tiger is yellow and black, etc. The other exam-

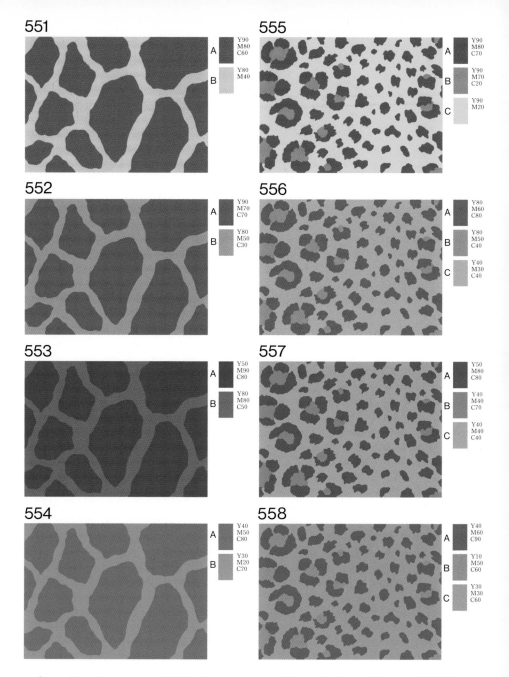

551

A — Y90 M80 C60

B — Y80 M40

555

A — Y90 M80 C70

B — Y90 M70 C20

C — Y90 M20

552

A — Y90 M70 C70

B — Y80 M50 C30

556

A — Y80 M60 C80

B — Y80 M50 C40

C — Y40 M30 C40

553

A — Y50 M90 C80

B — Y80 M80 C50

557

A — Y50 M80 C80

B — Y40 M40 C70

C — Y40 M40 C40

554

A — Y40 M50 C80

B — Y30 M20 C70

558

A — Y40 M60 C90

B — Y10 M50 C60

C — Y30 M30 C60

ples, colorwise, are pure fashion fantasy
— the chartreuse-and-black zebra (example 545), the blue-and-mauve leopard
(example 558). These and other, less
common animal prints — snake, dalma-
tion, pig, alligator, and pony — are so ap-

pealing and universally accepted that
they are as popular in unnatural as natural colors.

61

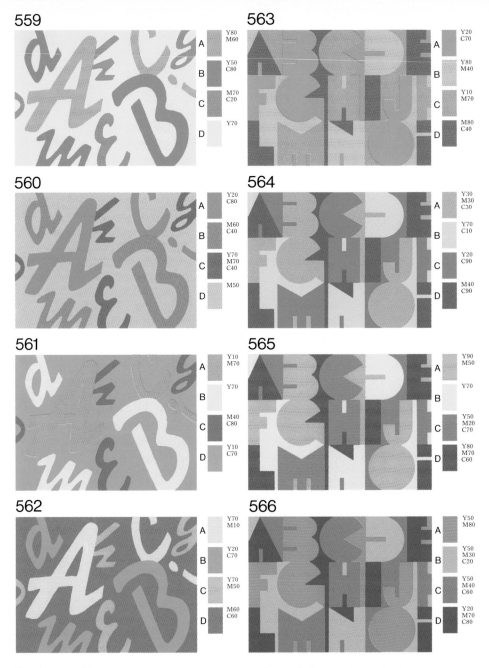

559

A Y80 M60
B Y50 C80
C M70 C20
D Y70

560

A Y20 C80
B M60 C40
C Y70 M70 C40
D M50

561

A Y10 M70
B Y70
C M40 C80
D Y10 C70

562

A Y70 M10
B Y20 C70
C Y70 M50
D M60 C60

563

A Y20 C70
B Y80 M40
C Y10 M70
D M80 C40

564

A Y30 M30 C30
B Y70 C10
C Y20 C90
D M40 C90

565

A Y90 M50
B Y70
C Y50 M20 C70
D Y80 M70 C60

566

A Y50 M80
B Y50 M30 C20
C Y50 M40 C60
D Y20 M70 C80

Numbers and Letters

In the four letter and number patterns shown here, a variety of type styles are used to create interesting design motifs. In examples 559-562, freely formed letters float on a soft pastel background to produce a bright and easy feminine image. The design in examples 563-566 is a puzzle of postmodern letters — a highly stylized alphabet that is barely recognizable within the gridlock, although contrasting colors help define the shapes.

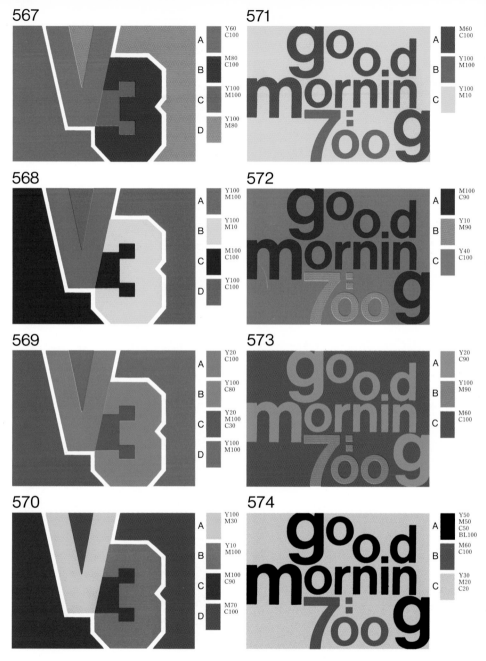

567

- A — Y60 C100
- B — M80 C100
- C — Y100 M100
- D — Y100 M80

571

- A — M60 C100
- B — Y100 M100
- C — Y100 M10

568

- A — Y100 M100
- B — Y100 M10
- C — M100 C100
- D — Y100 C100

572

- A — M100 C90
- B — Y10 M90
- C — Y40 C100

569

- A — Y20 C100
- B — Y100 C80
- C — Y20 M100 C30
- D — Y100 M100

573

- A — Y20 C90
- B — Y100 M90
- C — M60 C100

570

- A — Y100 M30
- B — Y10 M100
- C — M100 C90
- D — M70 C100

574

- A — Y50 M50 C50 BL100
- B — M60 C100
- C — Y30 M20 C20

The chromium colors in the supergraphics in examples 567-570 are made even brighter by the use of a white outline. The bold colors support the bold design. The Bauhaus type style in examples 571-574 has a contemporary feel, probably because of its use in public signs throughout Europe.

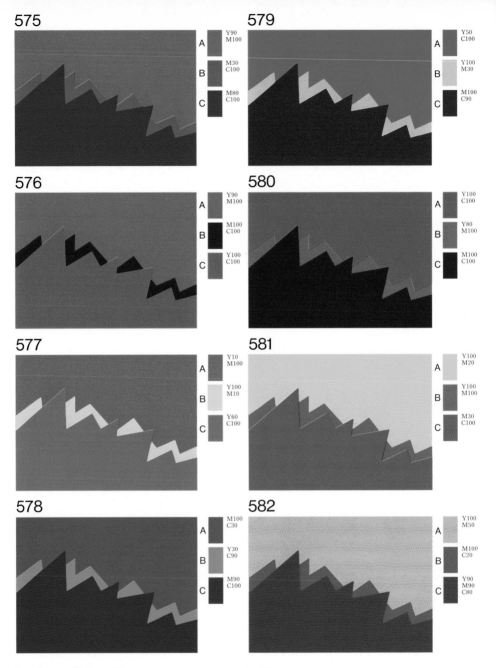

575

A — Y90 M100
B — M30 C100
C — M80 C100

579

A — Y50 C100
B — Y100 M30
C — M100 C90

576

A — Y90 M100
B — M100 C100
C — Y100 C100

580

A — Y100 C100
B — Y80 M100
C — M100 C100

577

A — Y10 M100
B — Y100 M10
C — Y60 C100

581

A — Y100 M20
B — Y100 M100
C — M30 C100

578

A — M100 C30
B — Y30 C90
C — M90 C100

582

A — Y100 M50
B — M100 C20
C — Y90 M90 C80

Landscape Prints: Mountains

This sharp-edged pattern resembles a mountain range cut from brightly colored paper. The key to this design is the B (connecting) color, which accents and gives each example a distinct personality. These compositions would change dramatically with a neutral — gray or beige — connecting color. The brilliant color palette intensifies the menacing character of the jagged peaks.

64

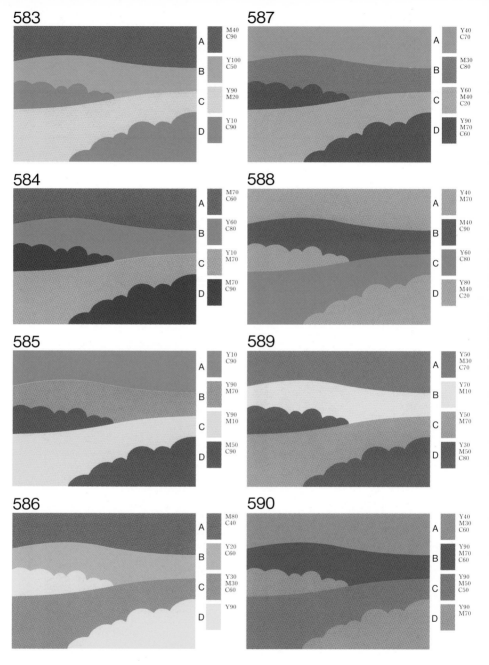

583

A M40 C90
B Y100 C50
C Y90 M20
D Y10 C90

587

A Y40 C70
B M30 C80
C Y60 M40 C20
D Y90 M70 C60

584

A M70 C60
B Y60 C80
C Y10 M70
D M70 C90

588

A Y40 M70
B M40 C90
C Y60 C80
D Y80 M40 C20

585

A Y10 C90
B Y90 M70
C Y90 M10
D M50 C90

589

A Y50 M30 C70
B Y70 M10
C Y50 M70
D Y30 M50 C80

586

A M80 C40
B Y20 C60
C Y30 M30 C60
D Y90

590

A Y40 M30 C60
B Y90 M70 C60
C Y90 M50 C50
D Y90 M70

Landscape Prints: Hills

This soft, undulating pattern brings to mind a simple landscape of hills, pathway, and sky. The colors used here, although gentler than those used in the previous mountain pattern, contrast suffi- ciently to define the different parts of the scene easily. Depending on how the brights (especially yellow) and darks are used, the motifs project or recede, thereby altering the perspective.

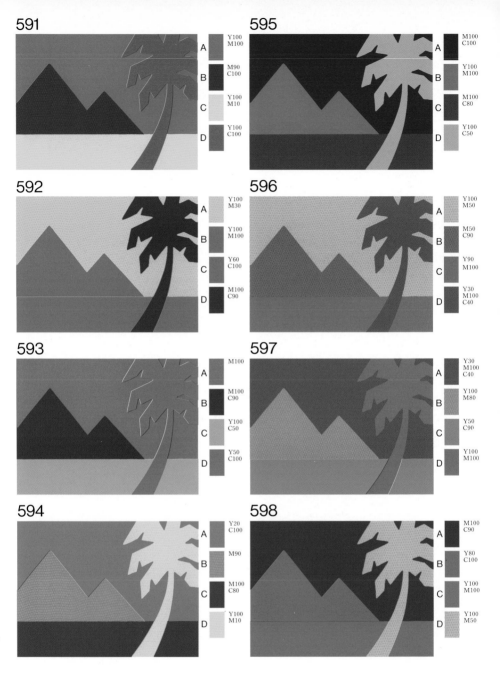

591

A	Y100 M100
B	M90 C100
C	Y100 M10
D	Y100 C100

595

A	M100 C100
B	Y100 M100
C	M100 C80
D	Y100 C50

592

A	Y100 M30
B	Y100 M100
C	Y60 C100
D	M100 C90

596

A	Y100 M50
B	M50 C90
C	Y90 M100
D	Y30 M100 C40

593

A	M100
B	M100 C90
C	Y100 C50
D	Y50 C100

597

A	Y30 M100 C40
B	Y100 M80
C	Y50 C90
D	Y100 M100

594

A	Y20 C100
B	M90
C	M100 C80
D	Y100 M10

598

A	M100 C90
B	Y80 C100
C	Y100 M100
D	Y100 M50

Landscape Prints: Pyramids

Only four colors are used in each of these examples to create a simple but striking design. Examples 591-594 each achieve ultimate contrast by mixing four maximum-color values together. The colors are slightly softer in examples 595-598 when the bright lemon yellow is replaced with gold orange. In examples 599-603, where earth colors are mixed

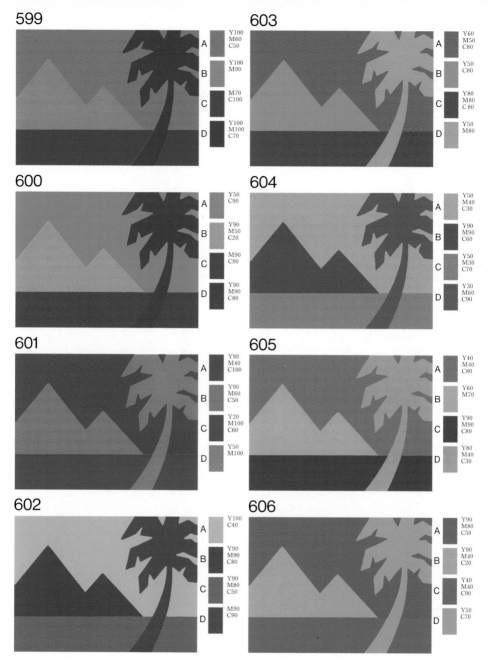

599

A	Y100 M60 C50
B	Y100 M90
C	M70 C100
D	Y100 M100 C70

603

A	Y60 M50 C80
B	Y50 C80
C	Y80 M80 C80
D	Y50 M80

600

A	Y50 C90
B	Y90 M50 C20
C	M90 C90
D	Y90 M90 C80

604

A	Y50 M40 C30
B	Y90 M90 C60
C	Y50 M30 C70
D	Y30 M60 C90

601

A	Y90 M40 C100
B	Y90 M60 C50
C	Y20 M100 C60
D	Y50 M100

605

A	Y40 M40 C80
B	Y60 M70
C	Y90 M90 C80
D	Y80 M40 C30

602

A	Y100 C40
B	Y90 M90 C80
C	Y90 M80 C50
D	M90 C90

606

A	Y90 M80 C50
B	Y90 M40 C20
C	Y40 M40 C90
D	Y50 C70

with brights, the brights dominate the composition and distort the perspective, as they did in the previous pattern. The feeling of the design changes completely in these four examples when the bright-

est hue is used to color a different motif. In examples 603-606, where neutrals are combined with medium pastels, the union is harmonious and visually appealing.

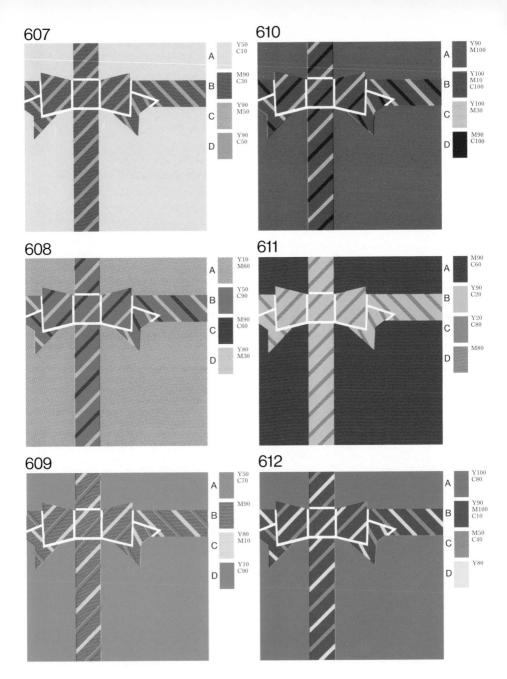

607

A	Y50 C10
B	M90 C30
C	Y90 M50
D	Y90 C50

610

A	Y90 M100
B	Y100 M10 C100
C	Y100 M30
D	M90 C100

608

A	Y10 M60
B	Y50 C90
C	M90 C60
D	Y80 M30

611

A	M90 C60
B	Y90 C20
C	Y20 C80
D	M80

609

A	Y50 C70
B	M90
C	Y80 M10
D	Y10 C90

612

A	Y100 C80
B	Y90 M100 C10
C	M50 C40
D	Y80

Children's Prints: Ribbons

This *trompe l'oeil* print changes personalities as it changes colors. Examples 607-609 are young and feminine, while examples 616-618 — despite the sweet brown motif — are older and masculine.

In all of these examples, the A (background) color is dominant but never overwhelms the motif colors. The B (bow) color sets the color mood of the design, which is lightened by the white accent. In most instances, complemen-

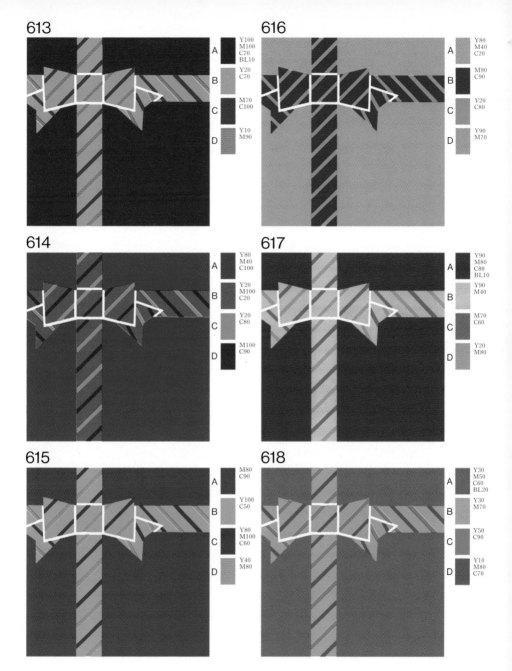

613

A — Y100 M100 C70 BL10
B — Y20 C70
C — M70 C100
D — Y10 M90

616

A — Y80 M40 C20
B — M90 C90
C — Y20 C80
D — Y90 M70

614

A — Y80 M40 C100
B — Y20 M100 C20
C — Y20 C80
D — M100 C90

617

A — Y90 M80 C80 BL10
B — Y90 M40
C — M70 C60
D — Y20 M80

615

A — M80 C90
B — Y100 C50
C — Y80 M100 C60
D — Y40 M80

618

A — Y30 M50 C60 BL20
B — Y30 M70
C — Y50 C90
D — Y10 M80 C70

tary or nearly complementary colors have been used in the bow to create a clean, graphic color statement.

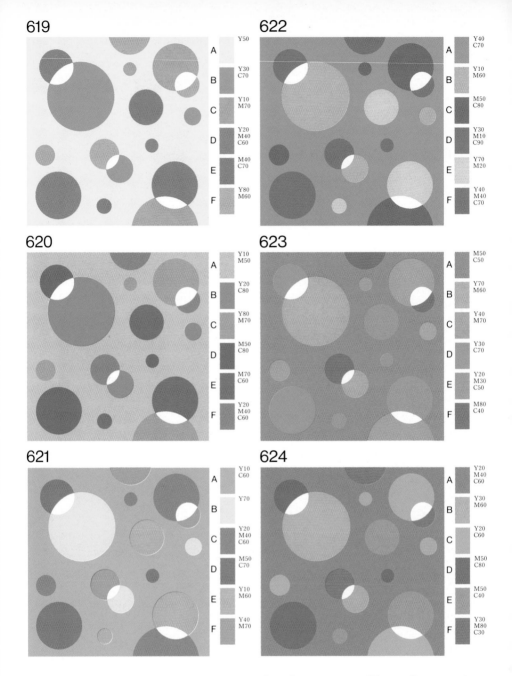

619

A · Y50
B · Y30 C70
C · Y10 M70
D · Y20 M40 C60
E · M40 C70
F · Y80 M60

622

A · Y40 C70
B · Y10 M60
C · M50 C80
D · Y30 M10 C90
E · Y70 M20
F · Y40 M40 C70

620

A · Y10 M50
B · Y20 C80
C · Y80 M70
D · M50 C80
E · M70 C60
F · Y20 M40 C60

623

A · M50 C50
B · Y70 M60
C · Y40 M70
D · Y30 C70
E · Y20 M30 C50
F · M80 C40

621

A · Y10 C60
B · Y70
C · Y20 M40 C60
D · M50 C70
E · Y10 M60
F · Y40 M70

624

A · Y20 M40 C60
B · Y30 M60
C · Y20 C60
D · M50 C80
E · M50 C40
F · Y30 M80 C30

Children's Prints: Soap Bubbles
This childlike design is reminiscent of
shiny soap bubbles floating languidly on
a pastel background. The strategic
placement of dark/light color contrasts
and the addition of white create the illu-
70

sion of transparency. The medium-pastel
and bright tones used in each example
give the design a bright, airy quality; the
consistent use of gray settles and calms
the composition.

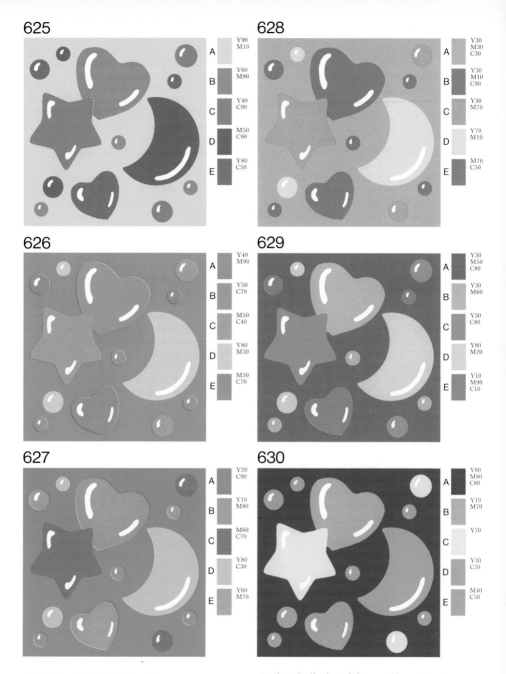

625

A	Y90 M10
B	Y60 M90
C	Y40 C90
D	M50 C90
E	Y80 C50

628

A	Y30 M30 C30
B	Y30 M10 C90
C	Y30 M70
D	Y70 M10
E	M70 C50

626

A	Y40 M90
B	Y50 C70
C	M50 C40
D	Y80 M30
E	M30 C70

629

A	Y30 M50 C80
B	Y30 M60
C	Y30 C80
D	Y80 M20
E	Y10 M90 C10

627

A	Y20 C90
B	Y10 M80
C	M60 C70
D	Y80 C30
E	Y60 M70

630

A	Y80 M80 C80
B	Y10 M70
C	Y70
D	Y30 C70
E	M40 C50

Children's Prints: Candies

These whimsical shapes, colored in bright pastels and white accents, resemble shiny hard candies. White keeps the design light and bright by modifying the otherwise heavy saturation of color due to the similarity of the motif and background colors. Example 630 is especially bright and clean because of the black background, which provides a highly contrasting base for the shining motifs.

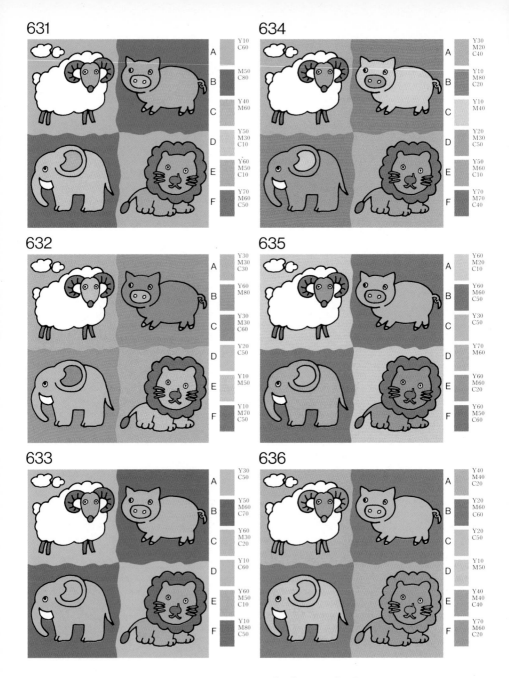

631

A	Y10 C60
B	M50 C80
C	Y40 M60
D	Y50 M30 C10
E	Y60 M50 C10
F	Y70 M60 C50

634

A	Y30 M20 C40
B	Y10 M80 C20
C	Y10 M40
D	Y20 M30 C50
E	Y50 M60 C10
F	Y70 M70 C40

632

A	Y30 M30 C30
B	Y60 M80
C	Y30 M30 C60
D	Y20 C50
E	Y10 M50
F	Y10 M70 C50

635

A	Y60 M20 C10
B	Y60 M60 C50
C	Y30 C50
D	Y70 M60
E	Y60 M60 C20
F	Y60 M50 C60

633

A	Y30 C50
B	Y50 M60 C70
C	Y60 M30 C20
D	Y10 C60
E	Y60 M50 C10
F	Y10 M80 C50

636

A	Y40 M40 C20
B	Y20 M60 C60
C	Y20 C50
D	Y10 M50
E	Y40 M40 C40
F	Y70 M60 C20

Children's Prints: Cartoon Animals

In a design appropriate for use in children's books and accessories, cartoon-like animals float in an *ichimatsu* check pattern. The check helps to organize an otherwise chaotic design, and the neu-tral colors used calm the composition. The thin black outline surrounding the simply drawn animals contributes to the cartoon feel of the pattern and supports the neutral color mood.

72

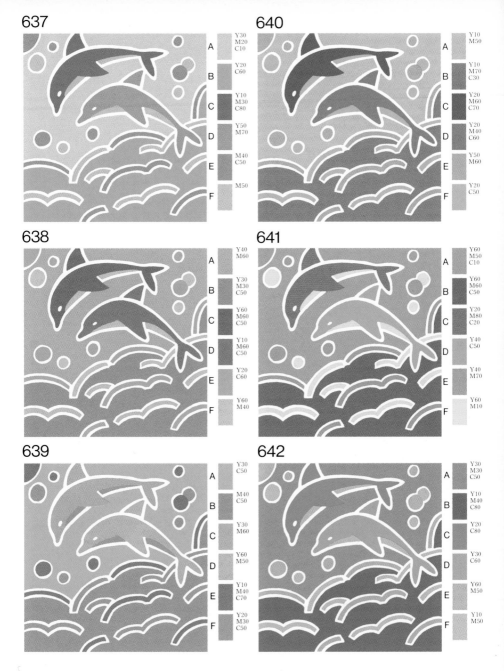

637

A	Y30 M20 C10
B	Y20 C60
C	Y10 M30 C80
D	Y50 M70
E	M40 C50
F	M50

640

A	Y10 M50
B	Y10 M70 C30
C	Y20 M60 C70
D	Y20 M40 C60
E	Y50 M60
F	Y20 C50

638

A	Y40 M60
B	Y30 M30 C50
C	Y60 M60 C50
D	Y10 M60 C50
E	Y20 C60
F	Y60 M40

641

A	Y60 M50 C10
B	Y60 M60 C50
C	Y20 M80 C20
D	Y40 C50
E	Y40 M70
F	Y60 M10

639

A	Y30 C50
B	M40 C50
C	Y30 M60
D	Y60 M50
E	Y10 M40 C70
F	Y20 M30 C50

642

A	Y30 M30 C50
B	Y10 M40 C80
C	Y20 C80
D	Y30 C60
E	Y60 M50
F	Y10 M50

Children's Prints: Dolphins

Somewhat similar to the soap bubble pattern on page 70, this spirited dolphin pattern uses bright neutrals to soften the design and a white outline to keep the color mood light and bright. The light colors used support the gaiety of the design, and the family color groups used in each of the examples keep the agitated imagery under control.

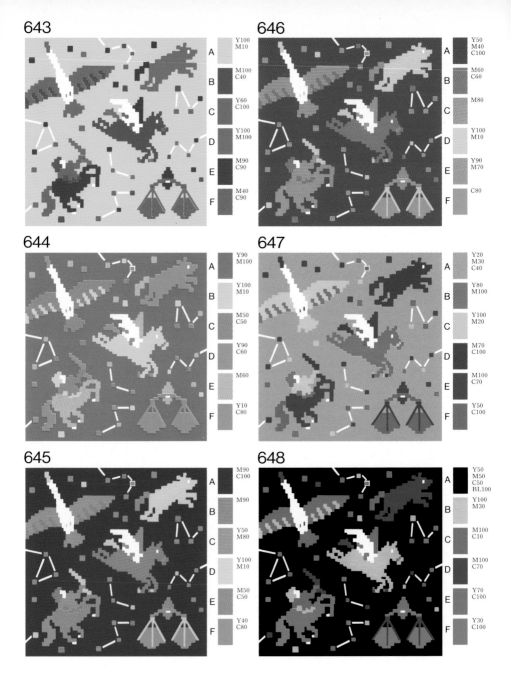

643

A	Y100 M10
B	M100 C40
C	Y60 C100
D	Y100 M100
E	M90 C90
F	M40 C90

646

A	Y50 M40 C100
B	M60 C60
C	M80
D	Y100 M10
E	Y90 M70
F	C80

644

A	Y90 M100
B	Y100 M10
C	M50 C50
D	Y90 C60
E	M60
F	Y10 C80

647

A	Y20 M30 C40
B	Y80 M100
C	Y100 M20
D	M70 C100
E	M100 C70
F	Y50 C100

645

A	M90 C100
B	M90
C	Y50 M80
D	Y100 M10
E	M50 C50
F	Y40 C80

648

A	Y50 M50 C50 BL100
B	Y100 M30
C	M100 C10
D	M100 C70
E	Y70 C100
F	Y30 C100

Children's Prints: Constellations

These fantasy motifs create a design perfect for young star gazers and appear to be charted—like a sweater or tapestry pattern—on a grid. The motifs are slightly abstracted, so the imagery works best when brightly colored motifs are placed on a neutral or black background (as in examples 647 and 648). Again, a bit of white brightens and freshens the design.

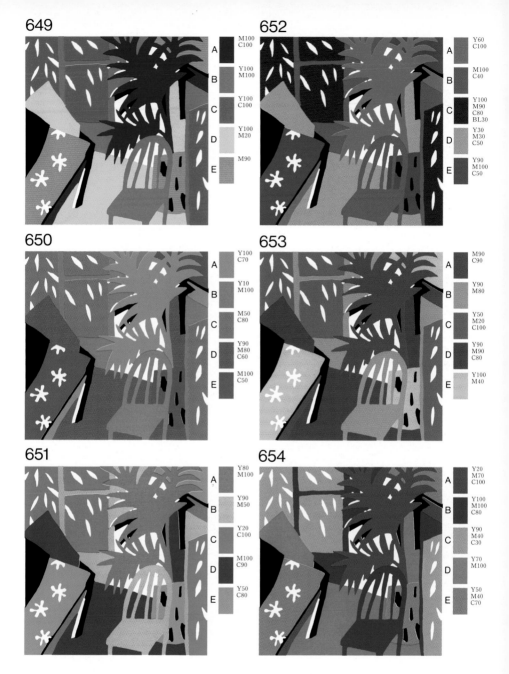

649

A	M100 C100
B	Y100 M100
C	Y100 C100
D	Y100 M20
E	M90

652

A	Y60 C100
B	M100 C40
C	Y100 M90 C80 BL30
D	Y30 M30 C50
E	Y90 M100 C50

650

A	Y100 C70
B	Y10 M100
C	M50 C80
D	Y90 M80 C60
E	M100 C50

653

A	M90 C90
B	Y90 M80
C	Y50 M20 C100
D	Y90 M90 C80
E	Y100 M40

651

A	Y80 M100
B	Y90 M50
C	Y20 C100
D	M100 C90
E	Y50 C80

654

A	Y20 M70 C100
B	Y100 M100 C80
C	Y90 M40 C30
D	Y70 M100
E	Y50 M40 C70

Interior Pattern

This interior print is taken from a painting by Matisse. Like the original work, bright tropical colors are mixed with brown, black, and white to create an atmosphere of sultry summer heat. Black and white keep the design controlled in a graphic sense — without them, the composition would be overwhelmed by the other colors, which are highly saturated.

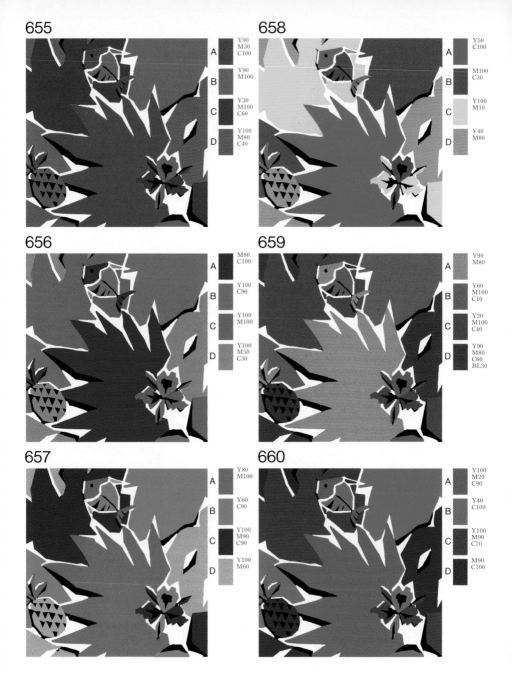

655

A	Y90 M30 C100
B	Y90 M100
C	Y30 M100 C60
D	Y100 M80 C40

658

A	Y50 C100
B	M100 C30
C	Y100 M10
D	Y40 M80

656

A	M80 C100
B	Y100 C90
C	Y100 M100
D	Y100 M50 C30

659

A	Y90 M80
B	Y60 M100 C10
C	Y20 M100 C40
D	Y90 M80 C60 BL30

657

A	Y80 M100
B	Y60 C90
C	Y100 M90 C90
D	Y100 M60

660

A	Y100 M20 C90
B	Y40 C100
C	Y100 M90 C70
D	M90 C100

Tropical Prints (1)

Tropical prints are perennial favorites and, like floral and animal prints, have a design category all their own. Examples 655-660, with their brilliance and jungle-like intensity, are typical of the bold tropical genre. The design motifs give the impression of being slightly off-register — this intentional arrangement allows the white background to peek through, keeping the design from becoming too intense.

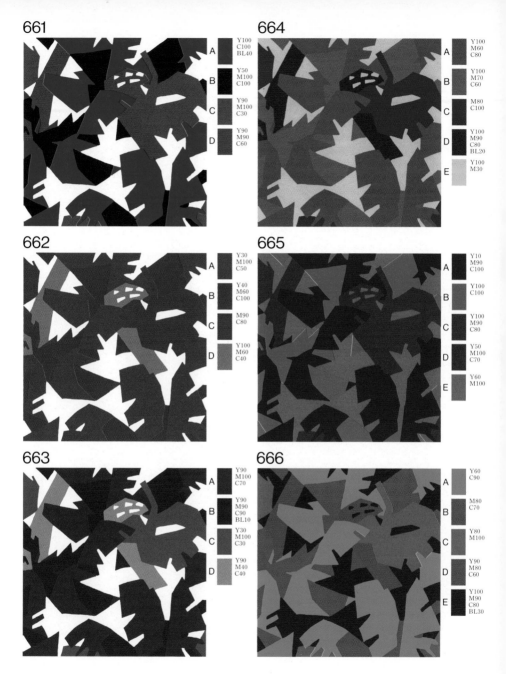

661

A	Y100 C100 BL40
B	Y50 M100 C100
C	Y90 M100 C30
D	Y90 M90 C60

664

A	Y100 M60 C80
B	Y100 M70 C60
C	M80 C100
D	Y100 M90 C80 BL20
E	Y100 M30

662

A	Y30 M100 C50
B	Y40 M60 C100
C	M90 C80
D	Y100 M60 C40

665

A	Y10 M90 C100
B	Y100 C100
C	Y100 M90 C80
D	Y50 M100 C70
E	Y60 M100

663

A	Y90 M100 C70
B	Y90 M90 C90 BL10
C	Y30 M100 C30
D	Y90 M40 C40

666

A	Y60 C90
B	M80 C70
C	Y80 M100
D	Y90 M80 C60
E	Y100 M90 C80 BL30

Tropical Prints (2)

These tropical prints show the different effects of using a white or a colored background. Examples 661-663, which use a white base, have a bright, clean summertime feeling. The dark-bright motifs produce color combinations that are upbeat without being juvenile. Examples 664-666, despite the bright colors, project a dark smothering of color. These colors en masse could be very oppressive.

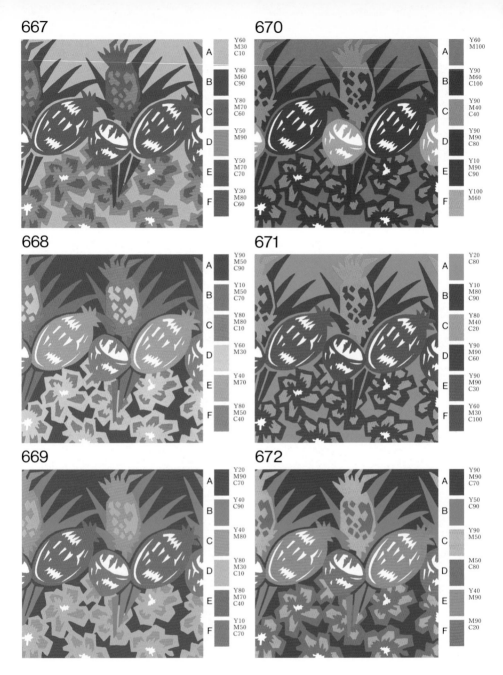

667

A	Y60 M30 C10
B	Y80 M60 C90
C	Y80 M70 C60
D	Y50 M90
E	Y50 M70 C70
F	Y30 M80 C60

670

A	Y60 M100
B	Y90 M60 C100
C	Y90 M40 C40
D	Y90 M90 C80
E	Y10 M90 C90
F	Y100 M60

668

A	Y90 M50 C90
B	Y10 M50 C70
C	Y80 M80 C10
D	Y60 M30
E	Y40 M70
F	Y80 M50 C40

671

A	Y20 C80
B	Y10 M80 C90
C	Y80 M40 C20
D	Y90 M90 C60
E	Y90 M90 C30
F	Y60 M30 C100

669

A	Y20 M90 C70
B	Y40 C90
C	Y40 M80
D	Y80 M30 C10
E	Y80 M70 C40
F	Y10 M50 C70

672

A	Y90 M90 C70
B	Y50 C90
C	Y90 M50
D	M50 C80
E	Y40 M90
F	M90 C20

Tropical Prints (3)

Styled to resemble a handmade woodcut print, this tropical print uses a close color range in each example that intensifies the abstract quality of the design. The white lightens the effect of the in- tense background colors. The design has a definite top and bottom. Such a di- rectional design is best used in wallpa- per and upholstery.

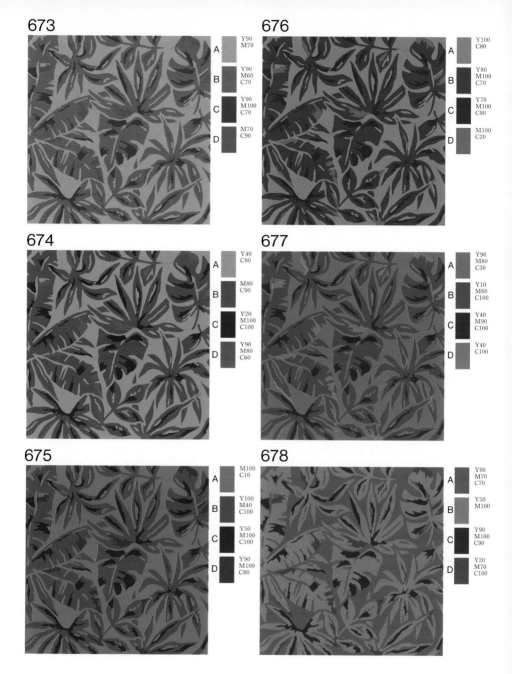

673

A	Y90 M70
B	Y90 M60 C70
C	Y90 M100 C70
D	M70 C90

676

A	Y100 C80
B	Y80 M100 C70
C	Y70 M100 C90
D	M100 C20

674

A	Y40 C80
B	M80 C90
C	Y20 M100 C100
D	Y90 M80 C60

677

A	Y90 M80 C30
B	Y10 M60 C100
C	Y40 M90 C100
D	Y40 C100

675

A	M100 C10
B	Y100 M40 C100
C	Y50 M100 C100
D	Y90 M100 C80

678

A	Y90 M70 C70
B	Y50 M100
C	Y90 M100 C90
D	Y20 M70 C100

Tropical Prints (4)

This print uses a little color trickery to create an exotic character. Although the pattern is crowded and tight, the design is not overwhelming because only two major colors (A and B) are used. The ac-cent colors (C and D) contrast with the main motifs and give them dimension and definition while brightening the composition as a whole.

79

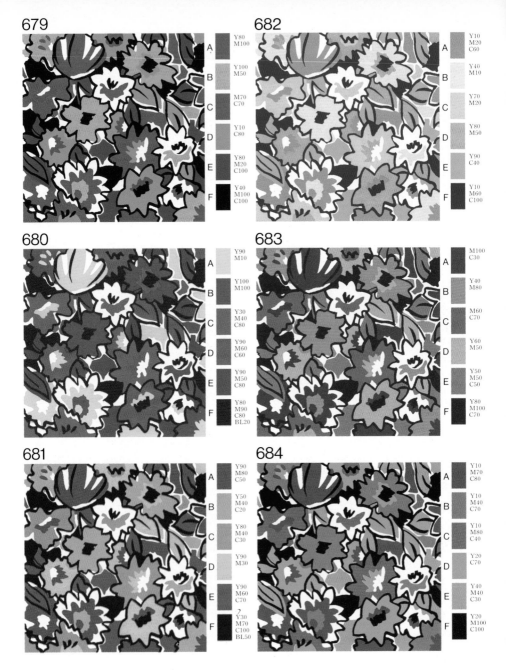

679

- A Y80 M100
- B Y100 M50
- C M70 C70
- D Y10 C80
- E Y80 M20 C100
- F Y40 M100 C100

682

- A Y10 M20 C60
- B Y40 M10
- C Y70 M20
- D Y80 M50
- E Y90 C40
- F Y10 M60 C100

680

- A Y90 M10
- B Y100 M100
- C Y30 M40 C80
- D Y90 M60 C60
- E Y90 M50 C80
- F Y80 M90 C80 BL20

683

- A M100 C30
- B Y40 M80
- C M60 C70
- D Y60 M50
- E Y50 M50 C50
- F Y80 M100 C70

681

- A Y90 M80 C50
- B Y50 M40 C20
- C Y80 M40 C30
- D Y90 M30
- E Y90 M60 C70
- F ? Y30 M70 C100 BL50

684

- A Y10 M70 C80
- B Y10 M40 C70
- C Y10 M80 C40
- D Y20 C70
- E Y40 M40 C30
- F Y20 M100 C100

Bouquet Floral Print

Floral patterns are the most popular print subjects. The variations and interpretations are endless, and entire industries were created to support the popularity of some of these styles. Liberty floral prints and William Morris designs are two of England's most important exports. The impressionistic wildflower design in examples 679-684 has a carefree personality encouraged by the use of medium-bright colors and white.

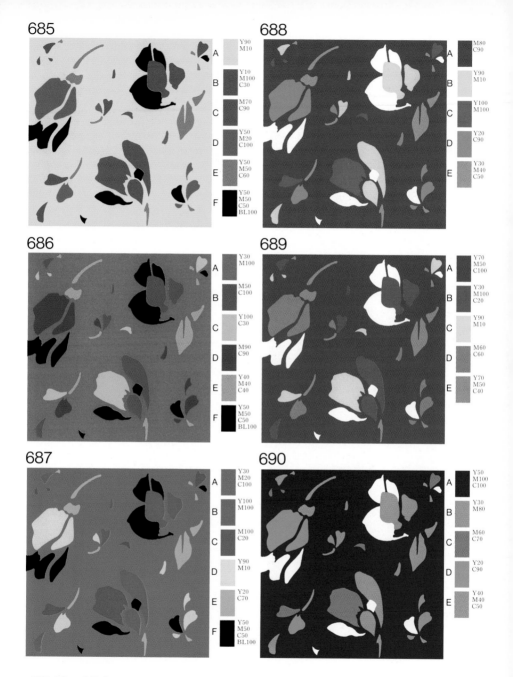

685

A	Y90 M10
B	Y10 M100 C30
C	Y70 C90
D	Y50 M20 C100
E	Y50 M50 C60
F	Y50 M50 C50 BL100

688

A	M80 C90
B	Y90 M10
C	Y100 M100
D	Y20 C90
E	Y30 M40 C50

686

A	Y30 M100
B	M50 C100
C	Y100 C30
D	M90 C90
E	Y40 M40 C40
F	Y50 M50 C50 BL100

689

A	Y70 M50 C100
B	Y30 M100 C20
C	Y90 M10
D	M60 C60
E	Y70 M50 C40

687

A	Y30 M20 C100
B	Y100 M100
C	M100 C20
D	Y90 M10
E	Y20 C70
F	Y50 M50 C50 BL100

690

A	Y50 M100 C100
B	Y30 M80
C	M60 C70
D	Y20 C90
E	Y40 M40 C50

Silk Floral Print

This simple abstract floral has a clean, contemporary look. The graphic quality of the design is due to the contrasting bright and dark colors. Black and white effectively create depth and dimension.

In examples 685-687, black contrasts with brilliant chromium backgrounds, and a neutral is added to soften the design. In examples 688-690, white petals contrast with the dark-bright background.

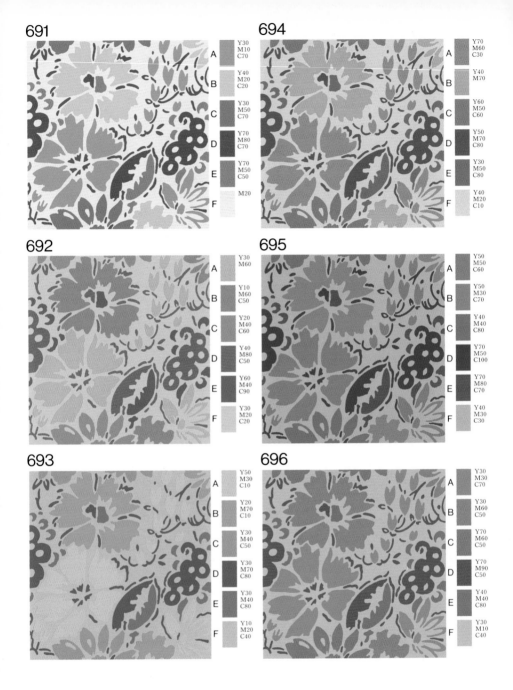

691

A — Y30 M10 C70
B — Y40 M20 C20
C — Y30 M50 C70
D — Y70 M80 C70
E — Y70 M50 C50
F — M20

694

A — Y70 M60 C30
B — Y40 M70
C — Y60 M50 C60
D — Y50 M70 C80
E — Y30 M50 C80
F — Y40 M20 C10

692

A — Y30 M60
B — Y10 M60 C50
C — Y20 M40 C60
D — Y40 M80 C50
E — Y60 M40 C90
F — Y30 M20 C20

695

A — Y50 M50 C60
B — Y50 M30 C70
C — Y40 M40 C80
D — Y70 M50 C100
E — Y70 M80 C70
F — Y40 M30 C30

693

A — Y50 M30 C10
B — Y20 M70 C10
C — Y30 M40 C50
D — Y30 M70 C80
E — Y30 M40 C80
F — Y10 M20 C40

696

A — Y30 M30 C70
B — Y30 M60 C50
C — Y70 M60 C50
D — Y70 M90 C50
E — Y40 M40 C80
F — Y30 M10 C40

Liberty Floral Print

Resembling a stenciled or woodcut pattern, this florid, intricate print is popular for interior use as upholstery or wall covering and is not usually found in clothing.

This pattern is often referred to as a *chintz print* because of the shiny finish the design can have on cloth. Examples 691-696 use pastels and soft brights; the neutrals and earth tones keep the image

82

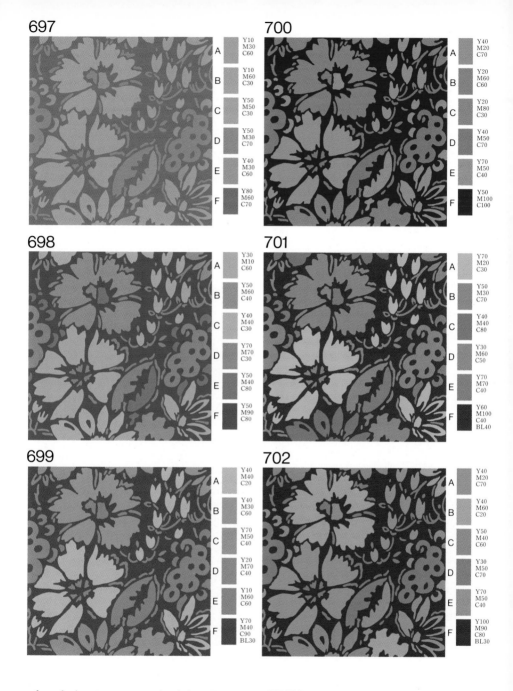

697

A	Y10 M30 C60
B	Y10 M60 C30
C	Y50 M50 C30
D	Y50 M30 C70
E	Y40 M30 C60
F	Y80 M60 C70

700

A	Y40 M20 C70
B	Y20 M60 C60
C	Y20 M80 C30
D	Y40 M50 C70
E	Y70 M50 C40
F	Y50 M100 C100

698

A	Y30 M10 C60
B	Y50 M60 C40
C	Y40 M40 C30
D	Y70 M70 C30
E	Y50 M40 C80
F	Y50 M90 C80

701

A	Y70 M20 C30
B	Y50 M30 C70
C	Y40 M40 C80
D	Y30 M60 C50
E	Y70 M70 C40
F	Y60 M100 C40 BL40

699

A	Y40 M40 C20
B	Y40 M30 C60
C	Y70 M50 C40
D	Y20 M70 C40
E	Y10 M60 C60
F	Y70 M40 C90 BL30

702

A	Y40 M20 C70
B	Y40 M60 C20
C	Y50 M40 C60
D	Y30 M50 C70
E	Y70 M50 C40
F	Y100 M90 C80 BL30

from being too sweet or feminine. The different shades of gray (C color) used in examples 691-694 refine the color composition and expand its versatility. The rich, sophisticated prints in examples 697-702 are evocative of Liberty florals. Examples 700-702 have a dusky beauty that is sharpened by the contrast of the dark background colors.

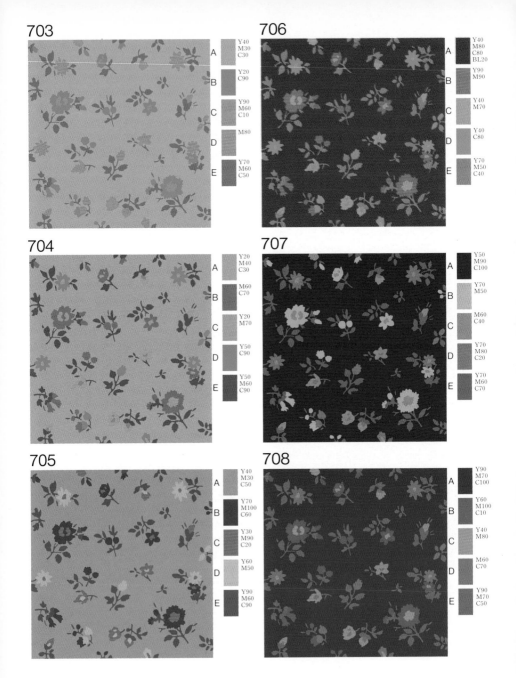

703

A — Y40 M30 C30
B — Y20 C90
C — Y90 M60 C10
D — M80
E — Y70 M60 C50

706

A — Y40 M80 C80 BL20
B — Y90 M90
C — Y40 M70
D — Y40 C80
E — Y70 M50 C40

704

A — Y20 M40 C30
B — M60 C70
C — Y20 M70
D — Y50 C90
E — Y50 M60 C90

707

A — Y50 M90 C100
B — Y70 M50
C — M60 C40
D — Y70 M80 C20
E — Y70 M60 C70

705

A — Y40 M30 C50
B — Y70 M100 C60
C — Y30 M90 C20
D — Y60 M50
E — Y90 M60 C90

708

A — Y90 M70 C100
B — Y60 M100 C10
C — Y40 M80
D — M60 C70
E — Y90 M70 C50

Wallpaper Floral Print

This pedestrian wallpaper floral is a classic print whose destiny is totally controlled by the background color. White, pastel, or bright backgrounds make the pattern suitable for children's clothing. A neutral base (examples 703-705) perfectly suits bedroom wall covering and upholstery. The dark background in examples 706-708 keeps the design from being to prissy and makes it acceptable for adult clothing.

84

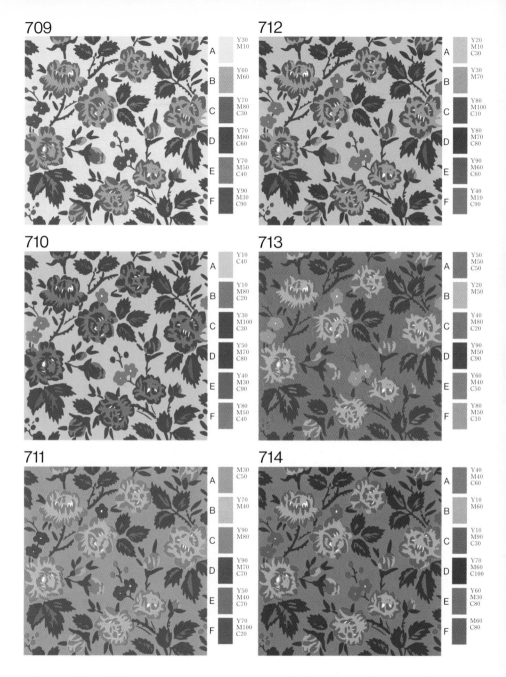

Rococo Floral Print

This rococo rose, an elegant design perfectly suited for use in upholstery and wall coverings, acquires depth through the juxtaposition of weak and strong colors. Each example uses tonal contrasts in the rose motif to make the rose look almost three-dimensional — in example 714, the B color is light rose, the C color is dark rose. This multidimensional impression deepens with a neutral gray background.

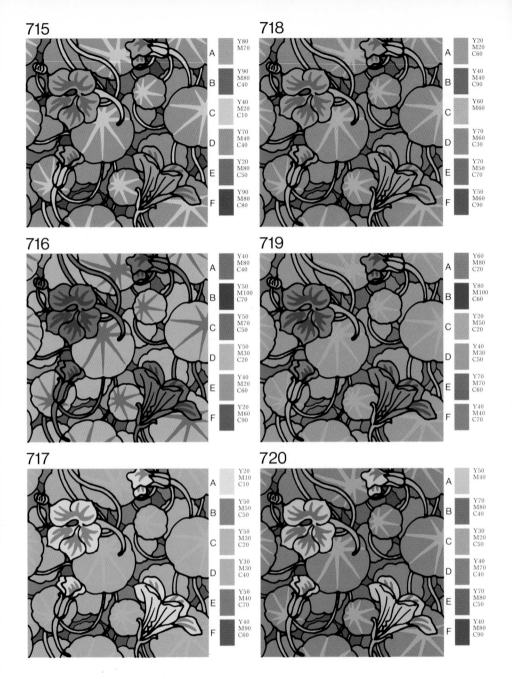

Art Nouveau Lilies

This ornate decorative style originated in Europe in the late nineteenth century and was made popular by the proliferation of William Morris prints and textiles. Art nouveau prints consist almost exclusively of floral subjects — lilies, thistles, undulating vines. Elegant curves prevail and, as in examples 715-720, natural colors mix with exotic oriental tones to give the design a dusky, mysterious air.

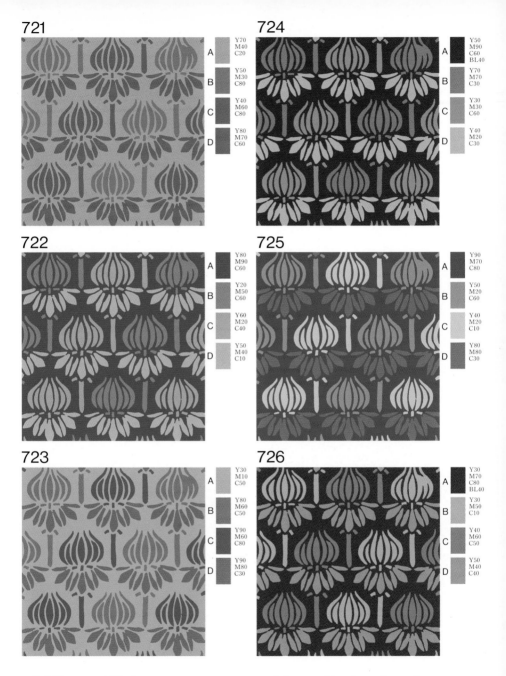

721

A	Y70 M40 C20
B	Y50 M30 C80
C	Y40 M60 C80
D	Y80 M70 C60

724

A	Y50 M90 C60 BL40
B	Y70 M70 C30
C	Y30 M30 C60
D	Y40 M20 C30

722

A	Y80 M90 C60
B	Y20 M50 C60
C	Y60 M20 C40
D	Y50 M40 C10

725

A	Y90 M70 C80
B	Y50 M20 C60
C	Y40 M20 C10
D	Y80 M80 C30

723

A	Y30 M10 C50
B	Y80 M60 C50
C	Y90 M60 C80
D	Y90 M80 C30

726

A	Y30 M70 C80 BL40
B	Y30 M50 C10
C	Y40 M60 C50
D	Y50 M40 C40

Art Nouveau Thistles

The romantic quality of this thistle pattern makes it distinctively art nouveau, despite its difference from the previous design. This composition has a linear regularity controlled by the diagonal striping resulting from alternating two blossom colors. Examples 721-723 are bright because dark brights are used on a light background. Examples 722 and 724-726 have more depth because light brights are used on a dark background.

87

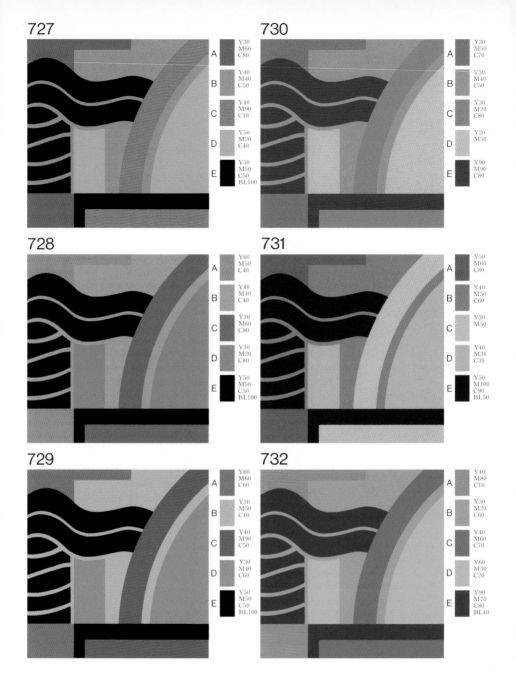

Art Deco Waves

Art deco became popular in the twenties and thirties, partly as a reaction to art nouveau — considered to be overly romantic — and partly in response to U.S. and European industrialization. Much modern design is based on this style, which had a tremendous influence on fashion, music, art, and interior and industrial design. Art deco, in contrast to art nouveau, uses cool, bold colors and emphasizes sharp, angular design.

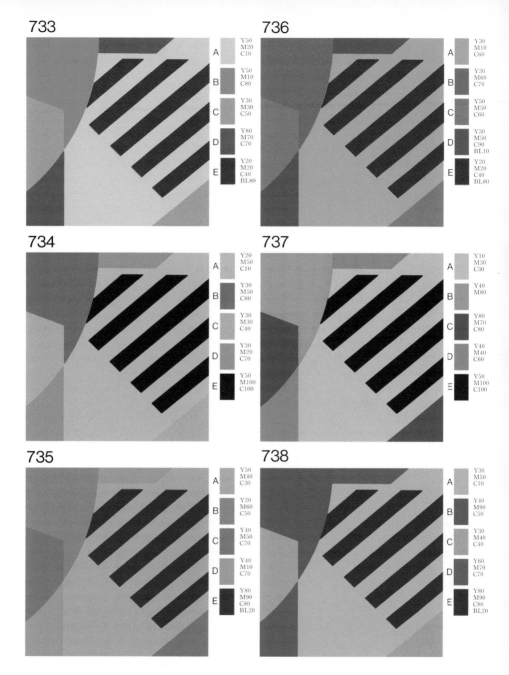

733

A	Y50 M20 C10
B	Y50 M10 C80
C	Y30 M30 C50
D	Y80 M70 C70
E	Y20 M20 C40 BL80

736

A	Y30 M10 C60
B	Y30 M60 C70
C	Y50 M50 C60
D	Y30 M50 C90 BL10
E	Y20 M20 C40 BL80

734

A	Y20 M50 C10
B	Y30 M50 C80
C	Y30 M30 C40
D	Y30 M20 C70
E	Y50 M100 C100

737

A	Y10 M30 C30
B	Y40 M80
C	Y80 M70 C80
D	Y40 M40 C60
E	Y50 M100 C100

735

A	Y50 M40 C30
B	Y20 M60 C50
C	Y40 M50 C70
D	Y40 M10 C70
E	Y80 M90 C80 BL20

738

A	Y30 M50 C10
B	Y40 M90 C50
C	Y30 M40 C40
D	Y60 M70 C70
E	Y80 M90 C80 BL20

Art Deco Stripes

Examples 733-738 clearly show art deco's emphasis on combining rhythmic curves and straight lines in one design. These examples are typical of textile designs created in the thirties. Tonal darks (rather than black) are used as the E color to dominate the bright pastel motifs. The gray and beige neutrals used throughout the pattern create an elegant, graceful impression that is also striking.

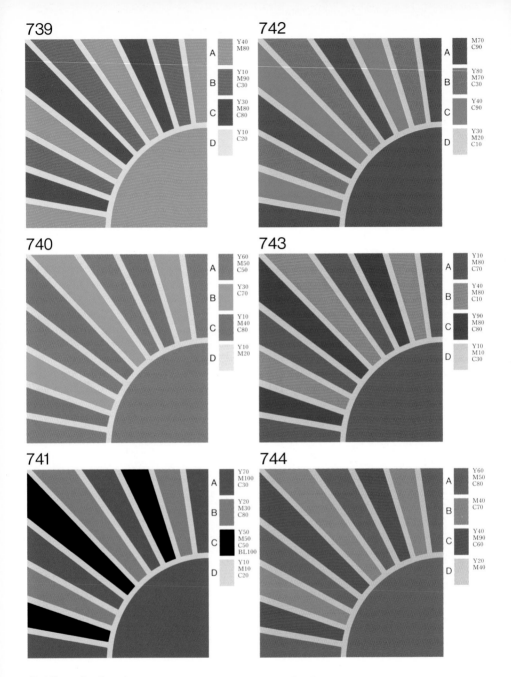

739

A — Y40 M80
B — Y10 M90 C30
C — Y30 M80 C80
D — Y10 C20

742

A — M70 C90
B — Y80 M70 C30
C — Y40 C90
D — Y30 M20 C10

740

A — Y60 M50 C50
B — Y30 C70
C — Y10 M40 C80
D — Y10 M20

743

A — Y10 M80 C70
B — Y40 M80 C10
C — Y90 M80 C80
D — Y10 M10 C30

741

A — Y70 M100 C30
B — Y20 M30 C80
C — Y50 M50 C50 BL100
D — Y10 M10 C20

744

A — Y60 M50 C80
B — M40 C70
C — Y40 M90 C60
D — Y20 M40

Art Deco Sunburst

A popular design theme in art deco, the sunburst permeates the textile and industrial art of the period. Because of its powerful simplicity, the design would succeed as a two-color print. These examples, however, use four colors and repeat the A (sun) color in the beam motif. The light outline brightens the image and contrasts with the darker tones to emphasize the radiant feeling of this design.

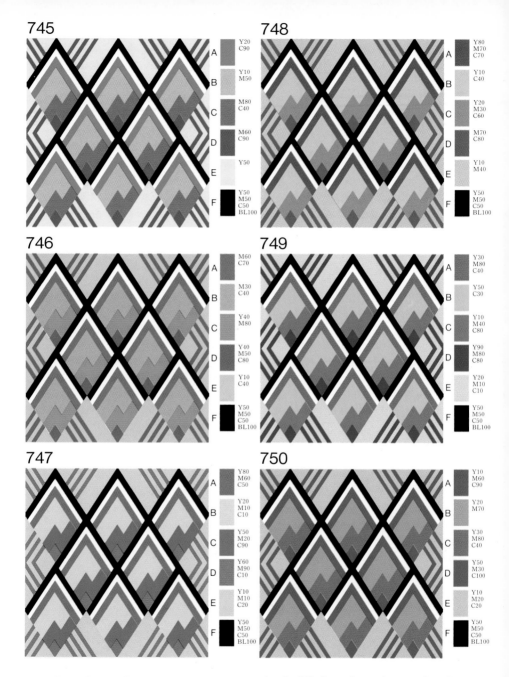

745

A	Y20 C90
B	Y10 M50
C	M80 C40
D	M60 C90
E	Y50
F	Y50 M50 C50 BL100

748

A	Y80 M70 C70
B	Y10 C40
C	Y20 M30 C60
D	M70 C80
E	Y10 M40
F	Y50 M50 C50 BL100

746

A	M60 C70
B	M30 C40
C	Y40 M80
D	Y40 M50 C80
E	Y10 C40
F	Y50 M50 C50 BL100

749

A	Y30 M80 C40
B	Y50 C30
C	Y10 M40 C80
D	Y90 M80 C80
E	Y20 M10 C10
F	Y50 M50 C50 BL100

747

A	Y80 M60 C50
B	Y20 M10 C10
C	Y50 M20 C90
D	Y60 M90 C10
E	Y10 M10 C20
F	Y50 M50 C50 BL100

750

A	Y10 M60 C90
B	Y20 M70
C	Y30 M80 C40
D	Y50 M30 C100
E	Y10 M20 C20
F	Y50 M50 C50 BL100

Art Deco Peacocks

Peacocks, an important theme in art nouveau, are interpreted here in an art deco pattern that hints at the op art movement yet to come. In these examples, peacock feathers are suggested by the black angles at the top of each diamond. The repetition of the diamond organizes the pattern. The use of black and white accentuates the sharp angles and light contrasts to make this a very powerful design.

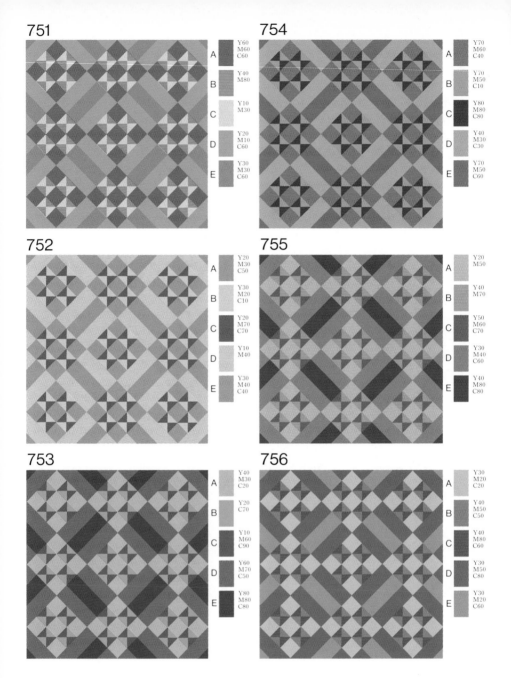

751

A	Y60 M60 C60
B	Y40 M80
C	Y10 M30
D	Y20 M10 C60
E	Y30 M30 C60

754

A	Y70 M60 C40
B	Y70 M50 C10
C	Y80 M80 C80
D	Y40 M30 C30
E	Y70 M50 C60

752

A	Y20 M30 C50
B	Y30 M20 C10
C	Y20 M70 C70
D	Y10 M40
E	Y30 M40 C40

755

A	Y20 M50
B	Y40 M70
C	Y50 M60 C70
D	Y30 M40 C60
E	Y40 M80 C80

753

A	Y40 M30 C20
B	Y20 C70
C	Y10 M60 C90
D	Y60 M70 C50
E	Y80 M80 C80

756

A	Y30 M20 C20
B	Y40 M50 C50
C	Y40 M80 C60
D	Y30 M50 C80
E	Y30 M20 C60

Mosaic Patterns (1)

The mosaic designs on the next six pages are similar to the quilt pattern designs shown previously — geometric pattern within geometric pattern within geometric pattern. These intricate tile patterns have ancient origins, and the variations on the design are almost infinite in the hands of a skilled artist. Examples 751-754 seem almost illumined because of the repetition of color contrasts in the design.

92

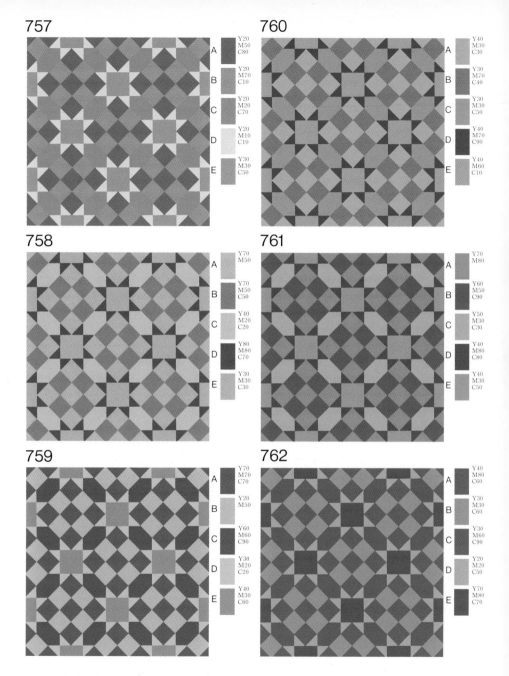

757

A	Y20 M50 C80
B	Y20 M70 C10
C	Y20 M20 C70
D	Y20 M10 C10
E	Y30 M30 C50

760

A	Y40 M30 C30
B	Y30 M70 C40
C	Y30 M30 C50
D	Y40 M70 C90
E	Y40 M60 C10

758

A	Y70 M50
B	Y70 M50 C50
C	Y40 M20 C20
D	Y80 M80 C70
E	Y30 M30 C30

761

A	Y70 M80
B	Y60 M50 C90
C	Y50 M30 C30
D	Y40 M80 C80
E	Y40 M30 C50

759

A	Y70 M70 C70
B	Y20 M50
C	Y60 M60 C90
D	Y30 M20 C20
E	Y40 M30 C60

762

A	Y40 M80 C60
B	Y30 M30 C60
C	Y30 M60 C90
D	Y20 M20 C50
E	Y70 M80 C70

Mosaic Patterns (2)

The feeling of any mosaic design depends greatly on color choice and juxtaposition. Examples 757-762 can be perceived in different ways — sometimes the star is visible, sometimes not.

In example 761, for example, where the D color is dark, the star is not easy to find. In examples 757 and 759, on the other hand, the star jumps out because the D color is light.

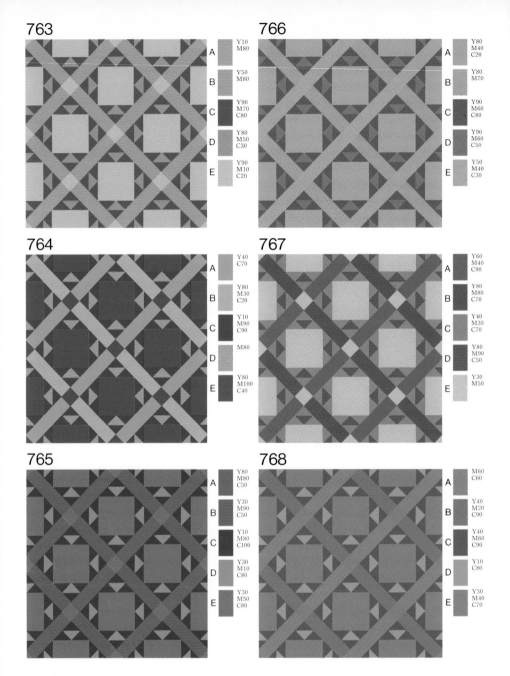

763

A	Y10 M80
B	Y50 M80
C	Y90 M70 C80
D	Y80 M50 C30
E	Y90 M10 C20

766

A	Y80 M40 C20
B	Y80 M70
C	Y90 M60 C80
D	Y90 M60 C50
E	Y50 M40 C30

764

A	Y40 C70
B	Y80 M30 C20
C	Y10 M90 C90
D	M80
E	Y80 M100 C40

767

A	Y60 M40 C90
B	Y80 M80 C70
C	Y40 M30 C70
D	Y80 M90 C50
E	Y30 M50

765

A	Y80 M80 C50
B	Y30 M90 C50
C	Y10 M80 C100
D	Y30 M10 C80
E	Y30 M50 C80

768

A	M60 C60
B	Y40 M20 C90
C	Y40 M60 C90
D	Y10 C80
E	Y30 M40 C70

Mosaic Patterns (3)

This checked mosaic, reminiscent of a quilting pattern, is extraordinary because of the unusual colors used — particularly in examples 763 and 767. Again, the personality of the design depends greatly on the choice of colors and their placement in the pattern. High contrasts emphasize the striping in examples 763, 764, 766, and 767. Examples 765 and 768 are more subdued and less jarring to the eye.

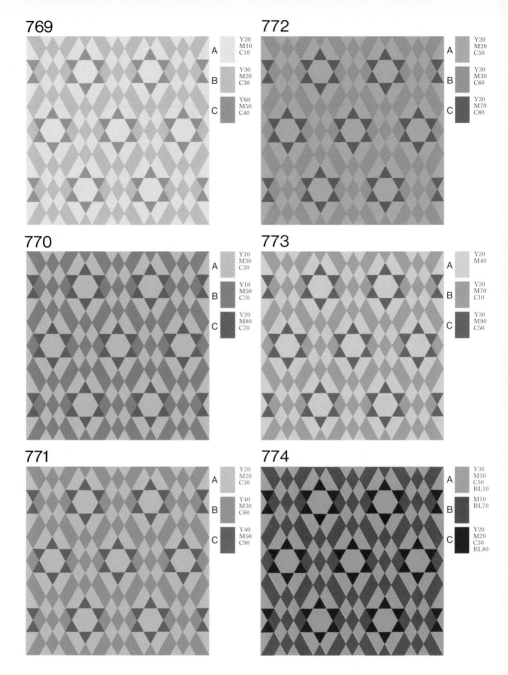

769

A — Y20 M10 C10
B — Y30 M20 C30
C — Y60 M50 C40

772

A — Y20 M20 C50
B — Y30 M30 C60
C — Y30 M70 C80

770

A — Y10 M30 C30
B — Y10 M50 C70
C — Y20 M80 C70

773

A — Y20 M40
B — Y20 M70 C10
C — Y30 M90 C50

771

A — Y20 M20 C30
B — Y40 M30 C60
C — Y40 M50 C90

774

A — Y30 M30 C30 BL10
B — M10 BL70
C — Y20 M20 C30 BL80

Mosaic Patterns (4)

In each of these subdued mosaics, slightly different values of the same color are used to produce a monotone effect. A complex mosaic design is easy to accept and appreciate when it is pre-sented in such a simple and accessible way. The design moves, but the visual shifts are minimal. A pattern in these un-demanding colors has wide appeal and would be perfect for flooring.

95

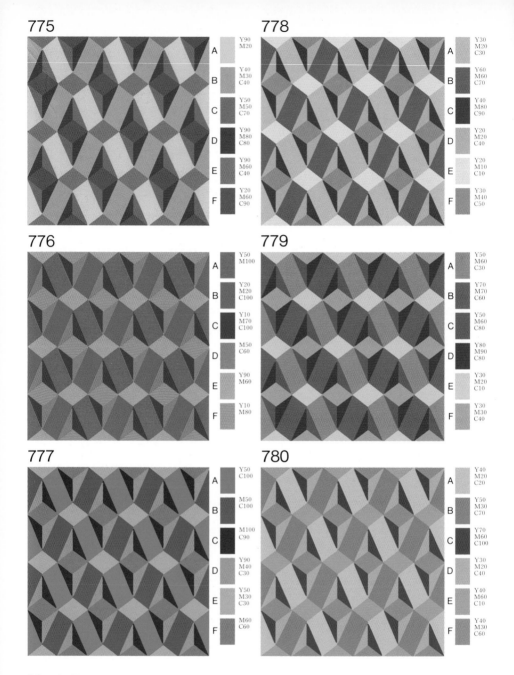

775

A		Y90 M20
B		Y40 M30 C40
C		Y50 M50 C70
D		Y90 M80 C80
E		Y90 M60 C40
F		Y20 M60 C90

778

A		Y30 M20 C30
B		Y60 M60 C70
C		Y40 M80 C90
D		Y20 M20 C40
E		Y20 M10 C10
F		Y30 M40 C50

776

A		Y50 M100
B		Y20 M20 C100
C		Y10 M70 C100
D		M50 C60
E		Y90 M60
F		Y10 M80

779

A		Y50 M60 C30
B		Y70 M70 C60
C		Y50 M60 C80
D		Y80 M90 C80
E		Y30 M20 C10
F		Y30 M30 C40

777

A		Y50 C100
B		M50 C100
C		M100 C90
D		Y90 M40 C30
E		Y50 M30 C30
F		M60 C60

780

A		Y40 M20 C20
B		Y50 M30 C70
C		Y70 M60 C100
D		Y30 M20 C40
E		Y40 M60 C10
F		Y40 M30 C60

Mosaic Patterns (5)

In an optical design that plays tricks on the eye, this powerful pattern seems to combine triangles and rectangles. In these examples, warm colors add a bright clarity and cool colors create shadows. As usual, the bright colors come forward and the dark colors sink. The complexity of the design is more palatable with closely related colors (examples 778-780) than with bright, garish combinations (examples 775-777).

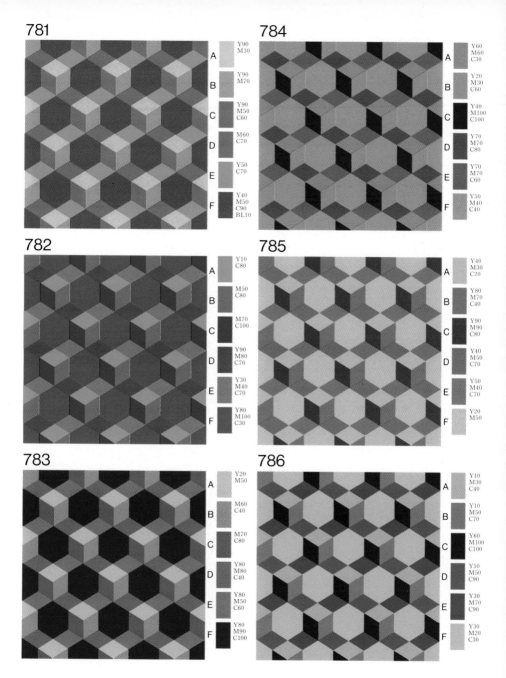

781

A — Y90 M30
B — Y90 M70
C — Y90 M50 C60
D — M60 C70
E — Y50 C70
F — Y40 M50 C90 BL10

784

A — Y60 M60 C30
B — Y20 M30 C60
C — Y40 M100 C100
D — Y70 M70 C80
E — Y70 M70 C60
F — Y50 M40 C40

782

A — Y10 C80
B — M50 C80
C — M70 C100
D — Y90 M80 C70
E — Y30 M40 C70
F — Y80 M100 C30

785

A — Y40 M30 C20
B — Y80 M70 C40
C — Y90 M90 C80
D — Y40 M50 C70
E — Y50 M40 C70
F — Y20 M50

783

A — Y20 M50
B — M60 C40
C — M70 C80
D — Y80 M80 C40
E — Y80 M50 C60
F — Y80 M90 C100

786

A — Y10 M30 C40
B — Y10 M50 C70
C — Y60 M100 C100
D — Y50 M50 C90
E — Y30 M70 C90
F — Y30 M20 C30

Mosaic Patterns (6)

This is another mosaic pattern in which the illusion of depth is created through the repetition of extreme color contrasts. The strong 3-D effect makes the cubes appear to be sitting alone, and not on a flat plane. The use of brights and medium brights as the A and E colors makes the pattern appear to move downward on the diagonal — except in example 785, where the F (pink) color creates a floating effect.

97

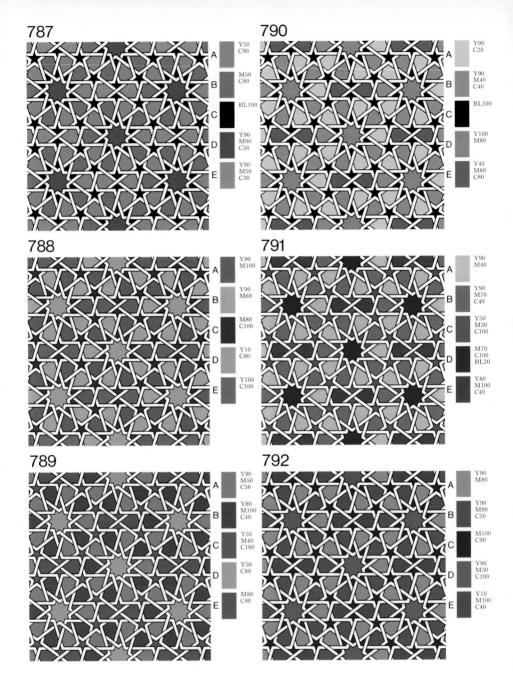

787

A	Y50 C90
B	M50 C80
C	BL100
D	Y90 M90 C50
E	Y90 M50 C30

790

A	Y90 C20
B	Y90 M40 C40
C	BL100
D	Y100 M80
E	Y40 M60 C80

788

A	Y90 M100
B	Y90 M60
C	M80 C100
D	Y10 C80
E	Y100 C100

791

A	Y90 M40
B	Y90 M70 C40
C	Y50 M30 C100
D	M70 C100 BL20
E	Y80 M100 C40

789

A	Y90 M50 C50
B	Y80 M100 C40
C	Y50 M40 C100
D	Y50 C80
E	M80 C80

792

A	Y90 M80
B	Y90 M90 C50
C	M100 C90
D	Y90 M30 C100
E	Y10 M100 C40

Islamic Patterns (1)

Related to mosaic patterns, these designs are taken from tile floor and wall patterns in ancient mosques and palaces. The star is very often the key to the designs, which are usually quite complex.

This particular design differs from the mosaics because the shapes used are not squares, rectangles, or triangles. In fact, the pattern appears to consist of an intricate web of faceted color.

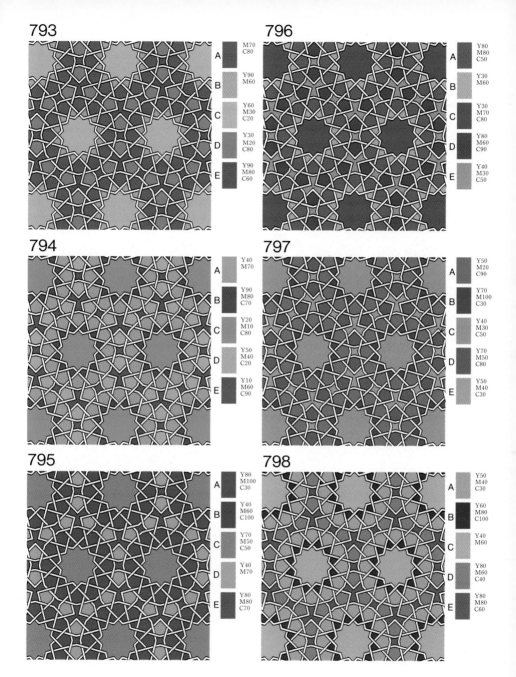

793

A	M70 C80
B	Y90 M60
C	Y60 M30 C20
D	Y30 M20 C80
E	Y90 M80 C60

796

A	Y80 M80 C50
B	Y30 M60
C	Y30 M70 C80
D	Y80 M60 C90
E	Y40 M30 C50

794

A	Y40 M70
B	Y90 M80 C70
C	Y20 M10 C80
D	Y50 M40 C20
E	Y10 M60 C90

797

A	Y50 M20 C90
B	Y70 M100 C30
C	Y40 M30 C50
D	Y70 M50 C80
E	Y50 M40 C30

795

A	Y80 M100 C30
B	Y40 M60 C100
C	Y70 M50 C50
D	Y40 M70
E	Y80 M80 C70

798

A	Y50 M40 C30
B	Y60 M80 C100
C	Y40 M60
D	Y80 M60 C40
E	Y80 M80 C60

Islamic Patterns (2)

In this second variation of the tile pattern, the colors used are typical of those found in actual tile works. In examples 793-798, the white outlines not only suggest plaster but also separate the colors to accentuate the star. The A color and B (star) color are always in high contrast to emphasize the design.

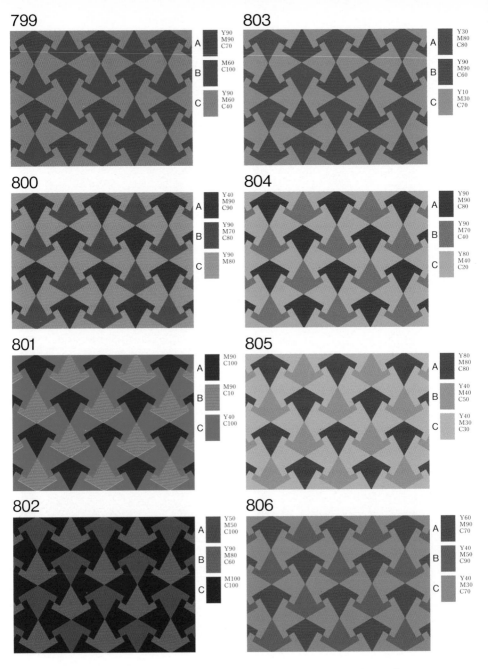

799

A — Y90 M90 C70
B — M60 C100
C — Y90 M60 C40

803

A — Y30 M80 C80
B — Y90 M90 C60
C — Y10 M30 C70

800

A — Y40 M90 C90
B — Y90 M70 C80
C — Y90 M80

804

A — Y90 M90 C80
B — Y90 M70 C40
C — Y80 M40 C20

801

A — M90 C100
B — M90 C10
C — Y40 C100

805

A — Y80 M80 C80
B — Y40 M40 C50
C — Y40 M30 C30

802

A — Y50 M50 C100
B — Y90 M80 C60
C — M100 C100

806

A — Y60 M90 C70
B — Y40 M50 C90
C — Y40 M30 C70

Islamic Patterns (3)

This very modern looking design is actually taken from a famous Islamic pattern at the Alhambra Palace in Granada, Spain. The graphic reinterpretation shows how contemporary design rede-

fines the past in fresh, innovative ways. The unusually shaped motif resembles a houndstooth but is more interesting. Light/dark contrasts manipulate the design; C is the base color because it appears twice as often as A or B.

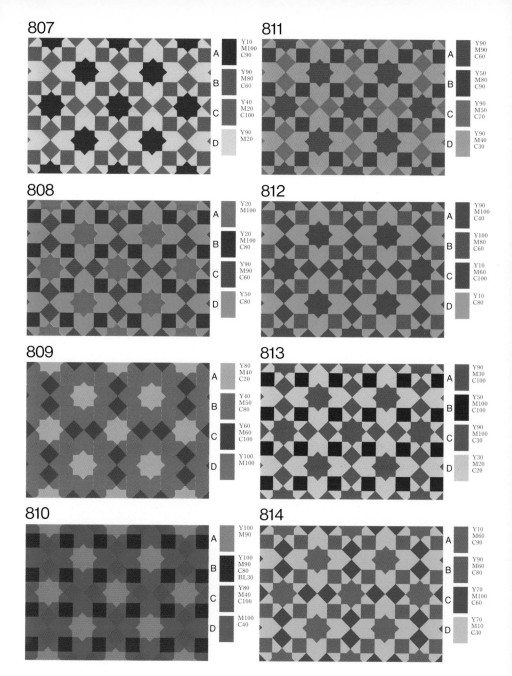

807

A — Y10 M100 C90
B — Y90 M80 C60
C — Y40 M20 C100
D — Y90 M20

808

A — Y20 M100
B — Y20 M100 C80
C — Y90 M90 C60
D — Y50 C80

809

A — Y80 M40 C20
B — Y40 M50 C80
C — Y60 M60 C100
D — Y100 M100

810

A — Y100 M90
B — Y100 M90 C80 BL30
C — Y80 M40 C100
D — M100 C40

811

A — Y90 M90 C60
B — Y50 M80 C90
C — Y90 M50 C70
D — Y90 M40 C30

812

A — Y90 M100 C40
B — Y100 M80 C60
C — Y10 M60 C100
D — Y10 C80

813

A — Y90 M30 C100
B — Y50 M100 C100
C — Y90 M100 C30
D — Y30 M20 C20

814

A — Y10 M60 C90
B — Y90 M60 C80
C — Y70 M100 C60
D — Y70 M10 C30

Islamic Patterns (4)

More conventional than the last design, this pattern is closer to mosaic tile patterns in feeling because of the square, diamond, and ubiquitous star motifs. The colors used here illustrate the exotic quality typical of all Islamic patterns. All sorts of combinations are used, but the A (star) color always contrasts with the D (background) color to ensure that the primary design motifs are sharp.

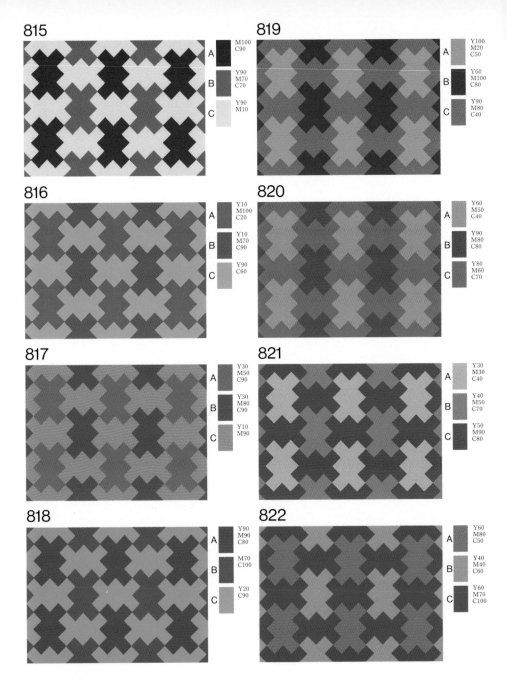

815

A	M100 C90
B	Y90 M70 C70
C	Y90 M10

819

A	Y100 M20 C50
B	Y60 M100 C80
C	Y90 M80 C40

816

A	Y10 M100 C20
B	Y10 M70 C90
C	Y90 C60

820

A	Y60 M50 C40
B	Y90 M80 C80
C	Y80 M60 C70

817

A	Y30 M50 C90
B	Y30 M80 C90
C	Y10 M90

821

A	Y30 M30 C40
B	Y40 M50 C70
C	Y50 M90 C80

818

A	Y90 M90 C80
B	M70 C100
C	Y20 C90

822

A	Y60 M80 C50
B	Y40 M40 C60
C	Y60 M70 C100

Islamic Patterns (5)

This pattern can be charted on a grid and is perfect for knits. Notice that the negative space (C color) has the same shape as the motifs. The original impression changes completely in examples
102

821 and 822, where the C color is darker than the motif colors — in examples 815-820, the diagonal is emphasized, while a strong horizontal-vertical direction prevails in examples 821 and 822.

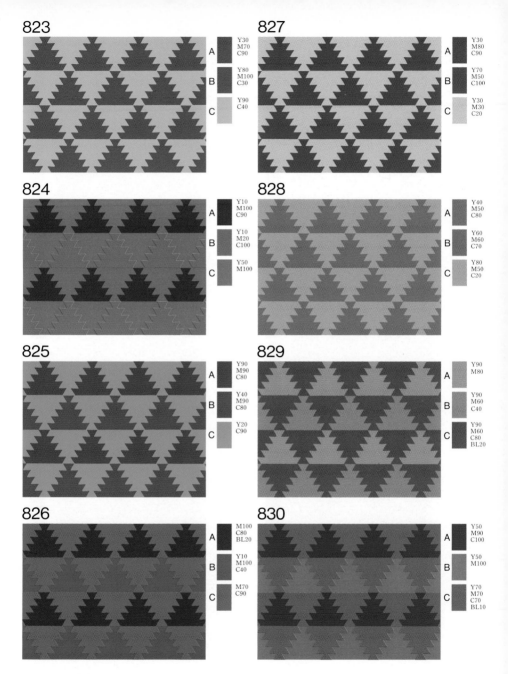

823

A	Y30 M70 C90
B	Y80 M100 C30
C	Y90 C40

827

A	Y30 M80 C90
B	Y70 M50 C100
C	Y30 M30 C20

824

A	Y10 M100 C90
B	Y10 M20 C100
C	Y50 M100

828

A	Y40 M50 C80
B	Y60 M60 C70
C	Y80 M50 C20

825

A	Y90 M90 C80
B	Y40 M90 C80
C	Y20 C90

829

A	Y90 M80
B	Y90 M60 C40
C	Y90 M60 C80 BL20

826

A	M100 C80 BL20
B	Y10 M100 C40
C	M70 C90

830

A	Y50 M90 C100
B	Y50 M100
C	Y70 M70 C70 BL10

Islamic Patterns (6)

This traditional zigzag-triangle pattern is often found on window and wall frames in Islamic mosques. The reinterpretation here is clean and stunning in its simplicity. The strong directional emphasis lim-

its the design's potential for textile use. High-contrast colors (examples 823, 824, and 827) give the composition a modern tone; related colors (example 826) give the design an ethnic quality.

103

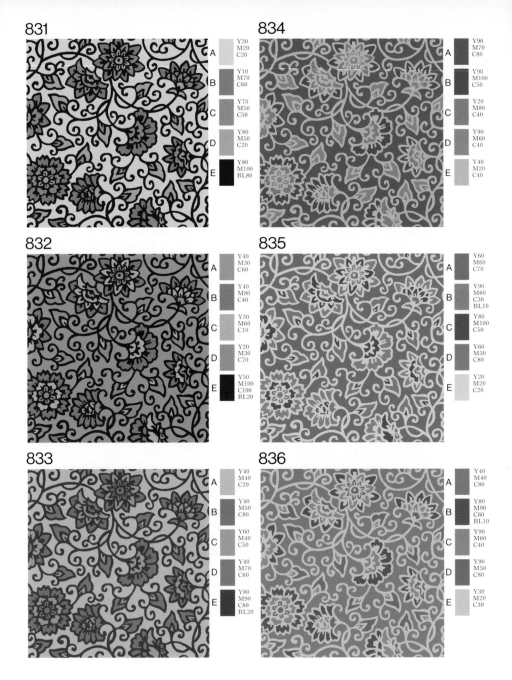

831

A	Y20 M20 C20
B	Y10 M70 C60
C	Y70 M50 C50
D	Y80 M50 C20
E	Y80 M100 BL80

834

A	Y90 M70 C80
B	Y90 M100 C50
C	Y20 M80 C40
D	Y90 M60 C40
E	Y40 M20 C40

832

A	Y40 M30 C60
B	Y40 M80 C40
C	Y30 M60 C10
D	Y20 M30 C70
E	Y50 M100 C100 BL20

835

A	Y60 M60 C70
B	Y90 M60 C30 BL10
C	Y80 M100 C50
D	Y60 M30 C80
E	Y20 M20 C20

833

A	Y40 M40 C20
B	Y40 M50 C80
C	Y60 M40 C50
D	Y40 M70 C60
E	Y80 M90 C80 BL20

836

A	Y40 M40 C80
B	Y80 M90 C60 BL10
C	Y90 M60 C40
D	Y90 M50 C80
E	Y30 M20 C30

Indian *Sarasa* Patterns (1)

Traditional Indian *Sarasa* patterns are woodcuts printed in natural vegetable colors and featuring intricate designs of plants, flowers, and birds. Examples 831-836 show a reinterpretation of a typical

Sarasa floral design. The colors used have a natural feeling and very much represent the color feeling of the originals, where natural dyes — similar in hue and harmony — are combined.

104

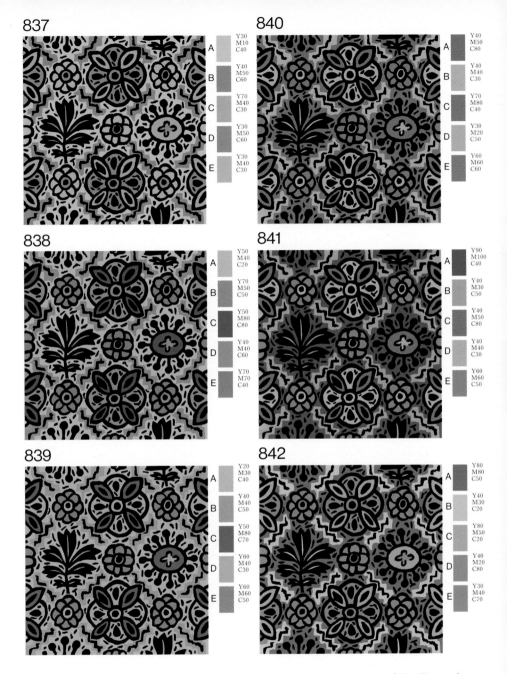

837

A	Y30 M10 C40
B	Y40 M50 C60
C	Y70 M40 C30
D	Y30 M50 C60
E	Y30 M40 C30

840

A	Y40 M50 C80
B	Y40 M40 C30
C	Y70 M80 C40
D	Y30 M20 C50
E	Y60 M60 C60

838

A	Y50 M40 C20
B	Y70 M50 C50
C	Y50 M80 C80
D	Y40 M40 C60
E	Y70 M70 C40

841

A	Y90 M100 C40
B	Y40 M30 C50
C	Y40 M50 C80
D	Y40 M40 C30
E	Y60 M60 C50

839

A	Y20 M30 C40
B	Y40 M40 C50
C	Y50 M80 C70
D	Y60 M40 C30
E	Y60 M60 C50

842

A	Y80 M80 C50
B	Y40 M30 C20
C	Y80 M50 C20
D	Y40 M20 C80
E	Y30 M40 C70

Indian *Sarasa* Patterns (2)

This *Sarasa* pattern also uses various vegetable color combinations. This design, however, introduces a heavy black outline, which accents the flower and leaf motifs and makes the pattern more graphic. The regularity of the diagonal check contributes to the boldness of the pattern. This geometry is apparent in examples 840-842, where the dark background color contrasts with the B color (the check outline).

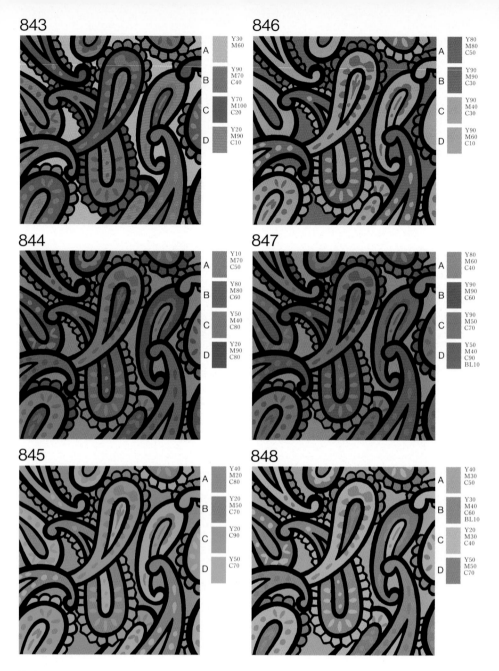

843

A	Y30 M60
B	Y90 M70 C40
C	Y70 M100 C20
D	Y20 M90 C10

846

A	Y80 M80 C50
B	Y90 M90 C30
C	Y90 M40 C30
D	Y90 M60 C10

844

A	Y10 M70 C50
B	Y80 M80 C60
C	Y50 M40 C80
D	Y20 M90 C80

847

A	Y80 M60 C40
B	Y90 M90 C60
C	Y90 M50 C70
D	Y50 M40 C90 BL10

845

A	Y40 M20 C80
B	Y20 M50 C70
C	Y20 C90
D	Y50 C70

848

A	Y40 M30 C50
B	Y30 M40 C60 BL10
C	Y20 M30 C40
D	Y50 M50 C70

Paisley Patterns (1)

Paisley patterns, like florals or stripes, have such broad appeal that they have their own category in the print world. This particular paisley is a stylized, contemporary version of the original design, which originated in the 18th century in the wool-producing town of Paisley, Scotland. The paisley print has regular surges of popularity that move this design classic to the fashion forefront.

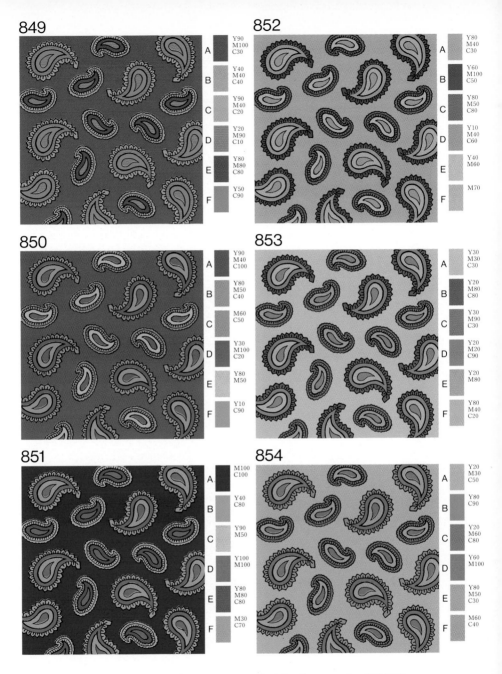

849

A	Y90 M100 C30
B	Y40 M40 C40
C	Y90 M40 C20
D	Y20 M90 C10
E	Y80 M80 C80
F	Y50 C90

852

A	Y80 M40 C30
B	Y60 M100 C50
C	Y80 M50 C80
D	Y10 M40 C60
E	Y40 M60
F	M70

850

A	Y90 M40 C100
B	Y80 M50 C40
C	M60 C50
D	Y30 M100 C20
E	Y80 M50
F	Y10 C90

853

A	Y30 M30 C30
B	Y20 M80 C80
C	Y30 M90 C30
D	Y20 M20 C90
E	Y20 M80
F	Y80 M40 C20

851

A	M100 C100
B	Y40 C80
C	Y90 M50
D	Y100 M100
E	Y80 M80 C80
F	M30 C70

854

A	Y20 M30 C50
B	Y80 C90
C	Y20 M60 C80
D	Y60 M100
E	Y80 M50 C30
F	M60 C40

Paisley Patterns (2)

This energetic, amoeba-like paisley relies on the dark outline to keep the design neat and precise. The scattered layout is typical of a paisley tie or shirt design. The rather non-traditional brights in examples 849-854 are very appealing. The high-contrast colors in the motifs highlight various parts of the pattern. Yellow, freely used throughout the examples, gives the design a bright feeling.

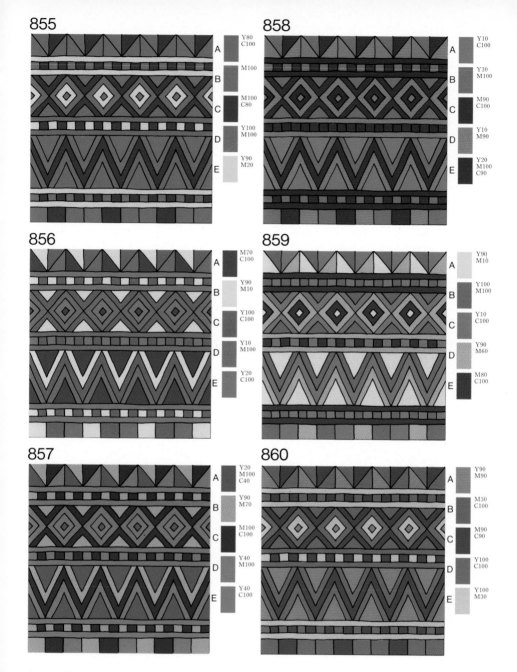

855

A	Y80 C100
B	M100
C	M100 C80
D	Y100 M100
E	Y90 M20

858

A	Y10 C100
B	Y30 M100
C	M90 C100
D	Y10 M90
E	Y20 M100 C90

856

A	M70 C100
B	Y90 M10
C	Y100 C100
D	Y10 M100
E	Y20 C100

859

A	Y90 M10
B	Y100 M100
C	Y10 C100
D	Y90 M60
E	M80 C100

857

A	Y20 M100 C40
B	Y90 M70
C	M100 C100
D	Y40 M100
E	Y40 C100

860

A	Y90 M90
B	M30 C100
C	M90 C90
D	Y100 C100
E	Y100 M30

Latin American Patterns (1)

The festive designs of Latin America are characterized by linear geometric patterns brightly colored in rainbow hues. Many traditional motifs are borrowed from Mayan and Aztec mythology. In ex- amples 855-860, the contrasting and complementary colors emphasize the strong geometry of the design. Although ancient in origin, these designs — with few changes to the originals — look sur- prisingly fresh and modern.

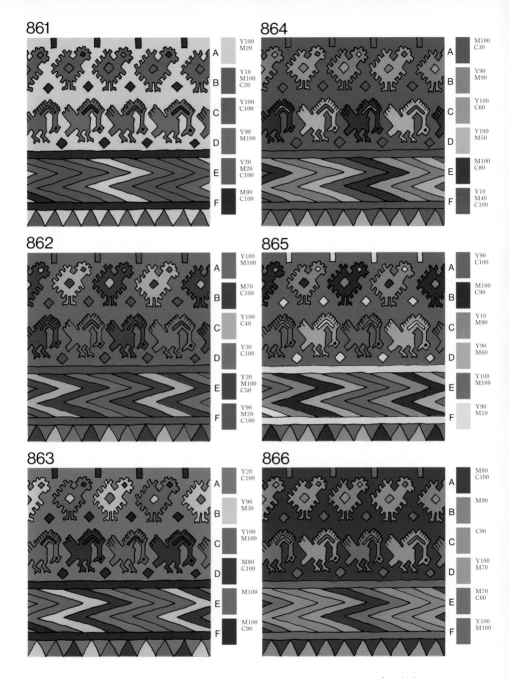

Latin American Patterns (2)

These animal motifs, while primitive in execution, are highly sophisticated in concept, and their cubist style suggests origins in woven textile patterns. The fiesta colors used are typical of South American weaving and painting — sour colors, juxtaposed with bright primary colors, heighten the brightness. Altogether, this eclectic mixture of color, motif, history, and geometry creates very provocative ethnic patterns.

109

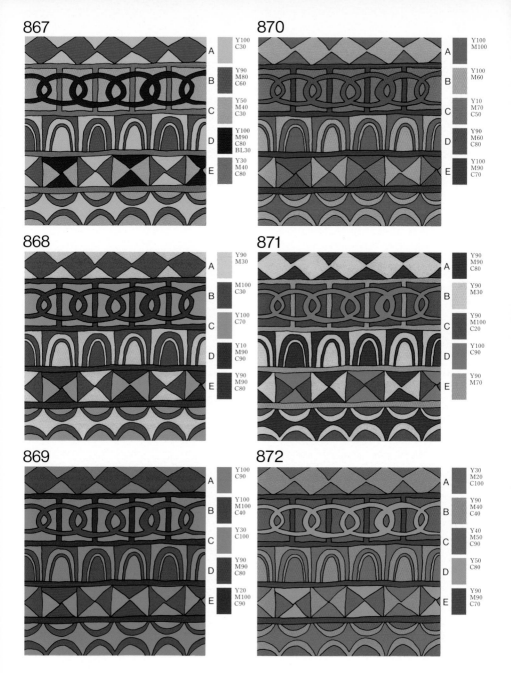

African Patterns (1)

Traditional African designs incorporate decorative design elements with ideograms (symbols that represent things or ideas). South American and African designs have many ties — both originate from ancient traditions; both are typically linear with an emphasis on geometric motifs. As examples 867-872 show, however, African designs are softer in shape and subtler in color.

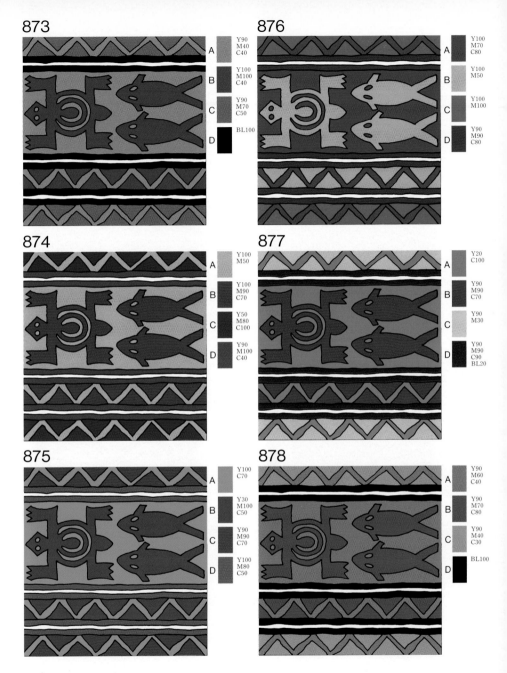

873

A	Y90 M40 C40
B	Y100 M100 C40
C	Y90 M70 C50
D	BL100

876

A	Y100 M70 C80
B	Y100 M50
C	Y100 M100
D	Y90 M90 C80

874

A	Y100 M50
B	Y100 M90 C70
C	Y50 M80 C100
D	Y90 M100 C40

877

A	Y20 C100
B	Y90 M90 C70
C	Y90 M30
D	Y90 M90 C90 BL20

875

A	Y100 C70
B	Y30 M100 C50
C	Y90 M90 C70
D	Y100 M80 C50

878

A	Y90 M60 C40
B	Y90 M70 C80
C	Y90 M40 C30
D	BL100

African Patterns (2)

This simple but powerful design uses symmetry to emphasize the primary design motifs — the turtle and fish. The deeply saturated colors used in examples 873-878 are heightened by the thin black outline and the off-white stripes. African designs often appear to be freely drawn, which gives them a freshness and a sense of humor. Having popular appeal, they are widely used in everything from interiors to clothing.

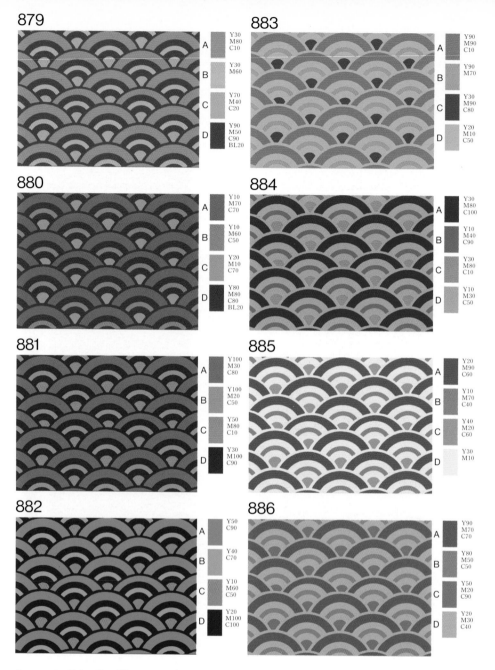

879

A — Y30 M80 C10
B — Y30 M60
C — Y70 M40 C20
D — Y90 M50 C90 BL20

880

A — Y10 M70 C70
B — Y10 M60 C50
C — Y20 M10 C70
D — Y80 M80 C80 BL20

881

A — Y100 M30 C80
B — Y100 M20 C50
C — Y50 M80 C10
D — Y30 M100 C90

882

A — Y50 C90
B — Y40 C70
C — Y10 M60 C50
D — Y20 M100 C100

883

A — Y90 M90 C10
B — Y90 M70
C — Y30 M90 C80
D — Y20 M10 C50

884

A — Y30 M80 C100
B — Y10 M40 C90
C — Y30 M80 C10
D — Y10 M30 C50

885

A — Y20 M90 C60
B — Y10 M70 C40
C — Y40 M20 C60
D — Y30 M10

886

A — Y90 M70 C70
B — Y80 M50 C50
C — Y50 M20 C90
D — Y20 M30 C40

Japanese *Seigaiha* (Blue Sea Wave)
The geometric half-circle appears in many cultures but is most important in Japanese tradition, where it is also known as a fish-scale pattern and used in kimono fabrics. In fabric design, the pattern is

usually colored in subtle gradations of a single hue. Examples 879-886, however, use strong color contrasts, emphasizing the individual parts of the design and creating an ebullience uncharacteristic of traditional kimono design.

112

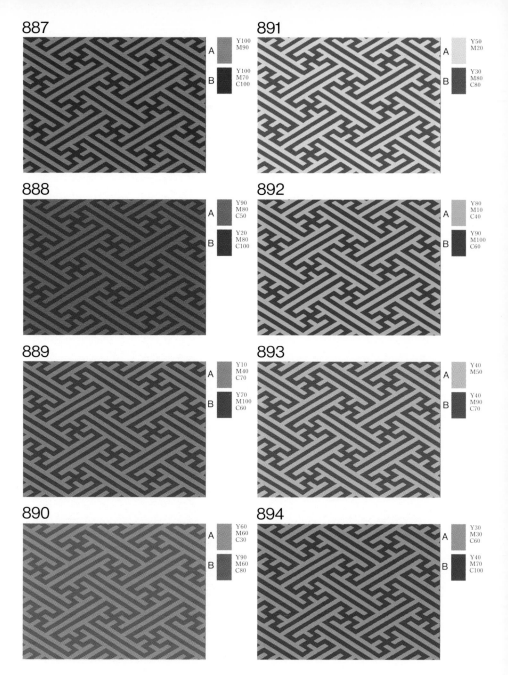

887

A Y100 M90
B Y100 M70 C100

888

A Y90 M80 C50
B Y20 M80 C100

889

A Y10 M40 C70
B Y70 M100 C60

890

A Y60 M60 C30
B Y90 M60 C80

891

A Y50 M20
B Y30 M80 C80

892

A Y80 M10 C40
B Y90 M100 C60

893

A Y40 M50
B Y40 M90 C70

894

A Y30 M30 C60
B Y40 M70 C100

Japanese *Sayagata* (Diamond) Pattern
Originally a woven pattern dating from
China's Ming dynasty, this classic design
is very popular in Japan and appears
often in Japanese textiles and pottery.
While the oriental feeling is intrinsic to

the design, the graphics are modern
and easily used in a contemporary occi-
dental context. As examples 887-894
show, the sophistication of the design
lends itself to interesting and unusual
color combinations.

113

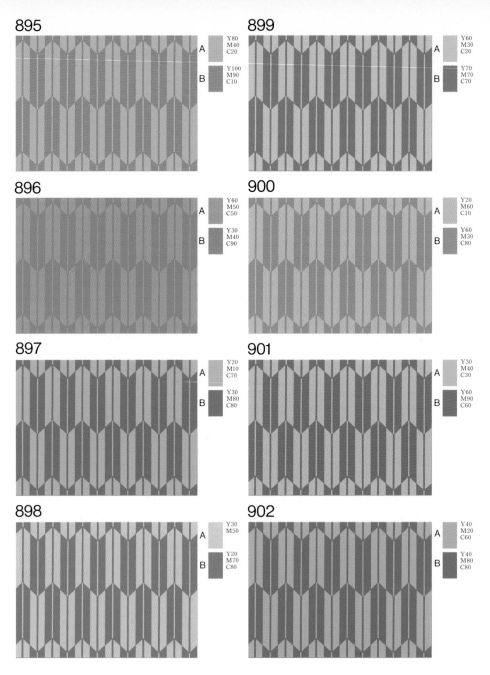

895

A Y80 M40 C20
B Y100 M90 C10

899

A Y60 M30 C20
B Y70 M70 C70

896

A Y60 M50 C50
B Y30 M40 C90

900

A Y20 M60 C10
B Y60 M30 C80

897

A Y20 M10 C70
B Y30 M80 C80

901

A Y30 M40 C30
B Y60 M90 C60

898

A Y30 M50
B Y20 M70 C80

902

A Y40 M20 C60
B Y40 M80 C80

Japanese *Yagasuri* (Arrow) Pattern
This arrow pattern, taken from traditional textile weaving, was often used in the court kimonos of early Japan and experienced a popular revival during Japan's Meiji era. In the original design, the ar-

row points used gradations of color, but this contemporary version uses sharp and clean contrasts. The design works horizontally or vertically and, depending on the direction selected, creates quite different effects.

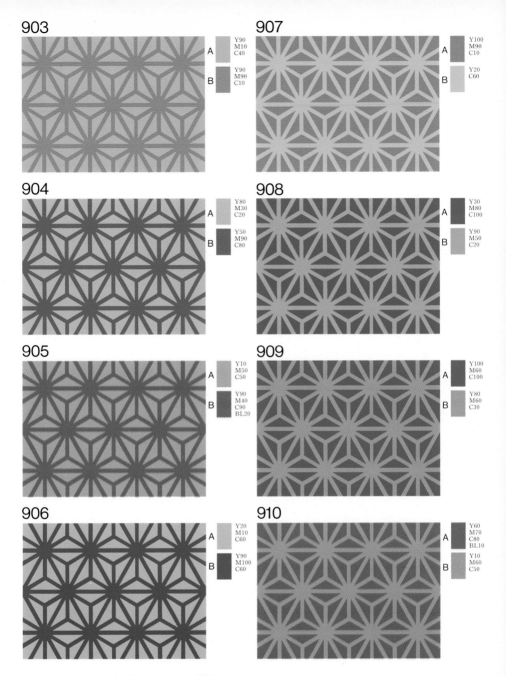

903

A — Y90 M10 C40

B — Y90 M90 C10

904

A — Y80 M30 C20

B — Y50 M90 C80

905

A — Y10 M50 C50

B — Y90 M40 C90 BL20

906

A — Y20 M10 C60

B — Y90 M100 C60

907

A — Y100 M90 C10

B — Y20 C60

908

A — Y30 M80 C100

B — Y90 M50 C20

909

A — Y100 M60 C100

B — Y80 M60 C30

910

A — Y60 M70 C80 BL10

B — Y10 M60 C50

Japanese *Asa No Ha* (Leaves of Hemp)
Westerners might interpret this design
as geometric, based on the hexagon.
The Japanese, however, relate the shape
to that of a hemp leaf and use the design
in children's wear as a symbol of

strength and growth. The examples have
different effects, depending on whether
the background is light or dark. Examples 903-906 are graphically pronounced,
while examples 907-910 have a luminos-
ity that dominates the design.

115

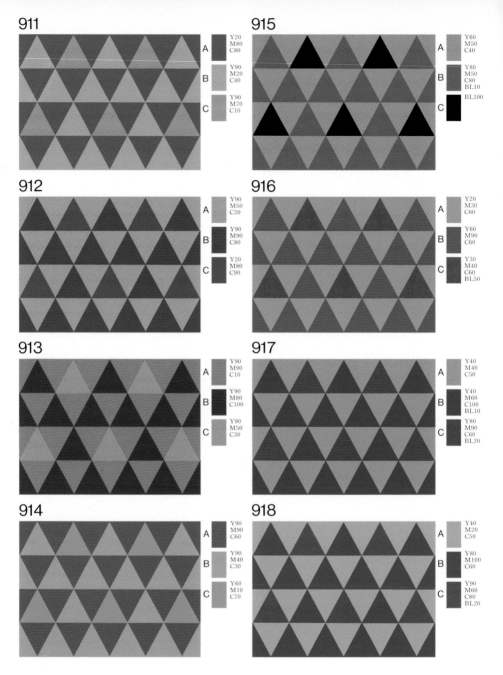

911

A	Y20 M80 C80
B	Y90 M20 C40
C	Y90 M70 C10

912

A	Y90 M50 C20
B	Y90 M90 C80
C	Y20 M80 C90

913

A	Y90 M90 C10
B	Y90 M80 C100
C	Y90 M50 C30

914

A	Y90 M90 C60
B	Y90 M40 C30
C	Y60 M10 C70

915

A	Y60 M50 C40
B	Y80 M50 C80 BL10
C	BL100

916

A	Y20 M30 C60
B	Y60 M90 C60
C	Y30 M40 C60 BL50

917

A	Y40 M40 C50
B	Y40 M60 C100 BL10
C	Y80 M90 C60 BL20

918

A	Y40 M20 C50
B	Y80 M100 C60
C	Y90 M60 C80 BL20

Japanese *Uroko* (Scale) Pattern

Similar to a quilt design, this contemporary triangle check is based on an ancient Japanese pattern that has been used in the traditional arts for centuries. Originally the design was used in theatrical clothing—as the harlequin check was—appearing in the costumes of the *Noh* dancers. Any color combinations work easily with this design, which uses the C color effectively as an accent.

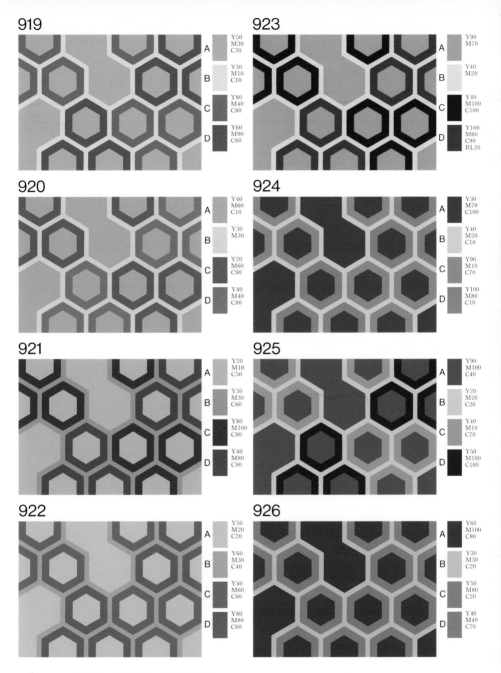

919

A	Y50 M30 C30
B	Y30 M10 C10
C	Y80 M40 C80
D	Y60 M90 C60

923

A	Y90 M70
B	Y40 M20
C	Y40 M100 C100
D	Y100 M60 C90 BL20

920

A	Y40 M60 C10
B	Y30 M30
C	Y20 M60 C90
D	Y40 M40 C80

924

A	Y30 M70 C100
B	Y40 M20 C10
C	Y90 M10 C70
D	Y100 M80 C10

921

A	Y20 M10 C50
B	Y30 M30 C60
C	Y80 M100 C80
D	Y40 M80 C90

925

A	Y90 M100 C40
B	Y20 M20 C20
C	Y40 M10 C70
D	Y50 M100 C100

922

A	Y50 M20 C20
B	Y60 M30 C40
C	Y40 M60 C80
D	Y80 M80 C60

926

A	Y60 M100 C80
B	Y30 M30 C20
C	Y50 M80 C20
D	Y40 M40 C70

Japanese *Kikkoh* (Turtle Shell) Pattern
In Japan, this series of hexagons is a celebratory symbol. The layout of the design can vary, but these examples maximize the base color, which dominates each composition. In most examples, a tone lighter than the background is used for the outline, which accents and defines the design. In examples 921-922, the outline is tonally darker than the base, creating soft, harmonious combinations.

117

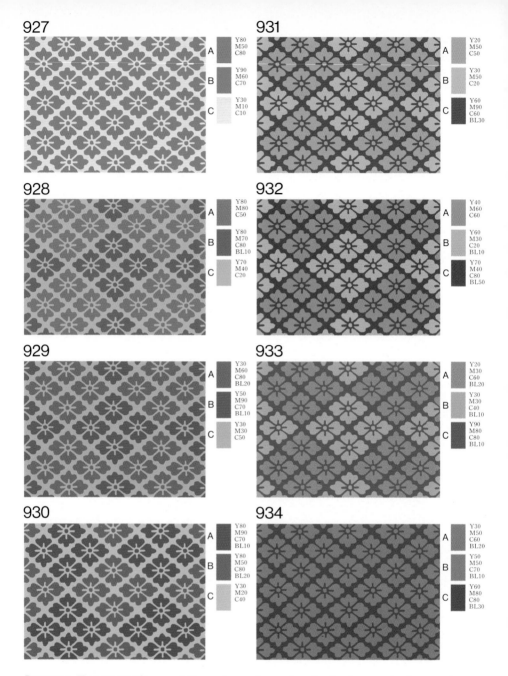

927

A Y80 M50 C80
B Y90 M60 C70
C Y30 M10 C10

928

A Y80 M80 C50
B Y80 M70 C80 BL10
C Y70 M40 C20

929

A Y30 M60 C80 BL20
B Y50 M90 C70 BL10
C Y30 M30 C50

930

A Y80 M90 C70 BL10
B Y80 M50 C80 BL20
C Y30 M20 C40

931

A Y20 M50 C50
B Y30 M50 C20
C Y60 M90 C60 BL30

932

A Y40 M60 C60
B Y60 M30 C20 BL10
C Y70 M40 C80 BL50

933

A Y20 M30 C60 BL20
B Y30 M30 C40 BL10
C Y90 M80 C80 BL10

934

A Y30 M50 C60 BL20
B Y50 M50 C70 BL10
C Y60 M80 C80 BL30

Japanese *Hanabishi* (Diamond-Shaped Flower) Pattern

This Japanese design is somewhat old-fashioned and is most often used in the kimonos of older women. The motif colors are suitably subtle and very much depend on the background colors used. The four petals of each flower are set in a diamond shape; then, four flowers repeat the configuration and form a larger diamond. The design uses alternating colors to create a checked pattern.

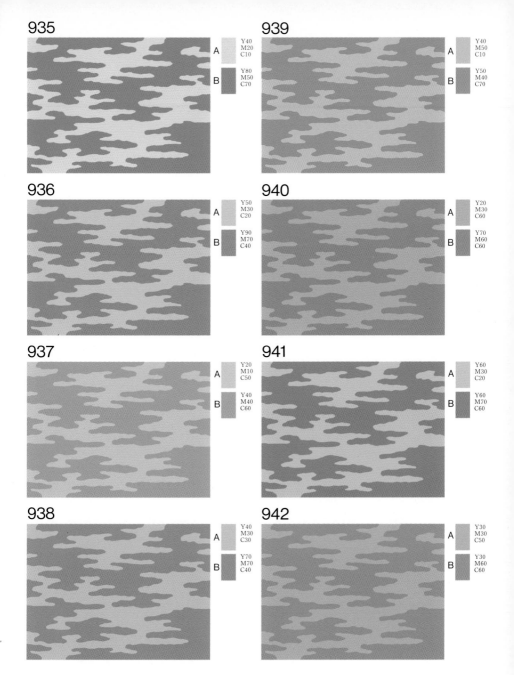

935

A — Y40 M20 C10
B — Y80 M50 C70

939

A — Y40 M50 C10
B — Y50 M40 C70

936

A — Y50 M30 C20
B — Y90 M70 C40

940

A — Y20 M30 C60
B — Y70 M60 C60

937

A — Y20 M10 C50
B — Y40 M40 C60

941

A — Y60 M30 C20
B — Y60 M70 C60

938

A — Y40 M30 C30
B — Y70 M70 C40

942

A — Y30 M30 C50
B — Y30 M60 C60

Japanese *Kuchiki Kumo* (Cloud-Shaped) Pattern

A popular design motif in Japan, cloud patterns appear not only in kimono art, but in woodwork, pottery, painting, and all areas of textile design — both ancient and contemporary. This particular interpretation has a simple, hand-drawn quality that flows easily, making base and motif difficult to tell apart. Closely or totally related colors contribute to the flowing character of the design.

119